THE BROADS
IN PRINT

A RETROSPECT
OF THE BOOKS & PAMPHLETS
PUBLISHED ABOUT THE NORFOLK
AND SUFFOLK BROADS

PART ONE:
THE DAYS OF DISCOVERY
THE EARLY 1800s TO 1920

David Clarke

ISBN 978 0 900616 86 0

Previously published
by the Author:

THE COUNTRY HOUSES OF NORFOLK
Part One: The Major Houses (2006)

THE COUNTRY HOUSES OF NORFOLK
Part Two: The Lost Houses (2008)

Part Three is now in preparation

Published by Joy and David Clarke,
The Elms, 19 Heigham Grove,
Norwich NR2 3DQ

Designed by Ashley Gray and Printed by Geo R Reeve Ltd,
9–11 Town Green, Wymondham, Norfolk NR18 0BD

CONTENTS

*Marsh Leaves by P H Emerson. The De Luxe edition
limited to 100 copies.*

INTRODUCTION

As a bookseller established for many years, one of my greatest pleasures was in swapping notes with our 'Broads' customers about the rarities and new discoveries in this field of collecting. Many only visited the shop at St Michael at Plea in Norwich (run by my wife Joy and myself) once or twice a year, often having travelled some distance, to sail or to hire a cruiser for a few days. Others, more locally based, we saw more frequently and they came in to keep an eye on what treasures we had unearthed. The question of why Geo Stephen's bibliography* had never been updated often came into the conversation – after all, as a collector, how do you know what to look out for when you don't know what exists in the first place!

My interest in books about the Broads came about as an adjunct to my researches into the development of the Norfolk and Suffolk tourist industry and, in particular, the stretch of coast that ran from Hunstanton down to Felixstowe. Many early coastal guides included a chapter about the Broads and the popularisation of this district became a fascination, leading to a comprehensive collection of books, ephemera and photographs, aided no doubt by the very fact that as a book dealer I generally had first choice of 'what came through the door'.

In this book I have not set out the chapters in an exact chronological order, but concentrate more on the writers and the content of their volumes rather than any strict time sequence. The appendix does give an attempt at a listing by date, however, I am certain that there is still scope for somebody to come forward and publish a far more exact and comprehensive bibliography of 'books published on the broads'.

Following my purchase at auction of a huge archive of books, articles and manuscripts by the Norfolk naturalist Arthur Patterson, which had been collected over many years by a Great Yarmouth bookseller, it is my intention in the future to publish a companion to this volume based on this fascinating character whose writings encompassed the natural history of

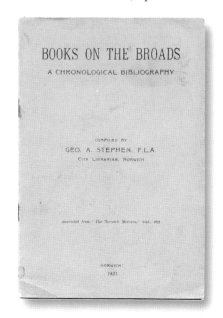

*Books on the Broads,
a chronological biography,
by Geo A Stephen.*

East Norfolk and the Broads but, as well, embraced such unrelated subjects as zoos, pet monkeys, shadow entertainments, truancy and goodness knows what else.

I would like to take this opportunity to record my thanks to Jean and Bernie Bobbin and to James Oxley-Brennan who permitted me to examine books in their possession, facilitating a more informed description of some of the titles within this text. I should also like to thank Ron Fiske with whom I share the passion of not only collecting Norfolk books, but also an interest in the people who wrote them and the history that they have unravelled. I greatly appreciated the opportunity to examine his library which led to several additional entries within this book. I would also like to thank my wife Joy, whose several readings of the manuscript helped prevent the more glaring errors that would otherwise be put before you in this book.

* Geo A Stephen, the then City Librarian, in 1921 published as a small booklet the first comprehensive 'stand alone' bibliography of Books on the Broads.

BEFORE THE TOURISTS

It was in the late 1870s when the 'father of broadland boat hire' John Loynes identified an opportunity to hire out boats for trips and holidays on Norfolk's rivers and broads, and by 1882 Jarrold & Sons had published the first edition of George Christopher Davies' *Handbook to the Rivers and Broads of Norfolk and Suffolk* which was to remain in print until the 1930s. It would, however, be wrong to think that the story of 'books about the Broads' only commenced at this time. Broadland boating holidays, albeit in a pioneering spirit, were undertaken as early as 1840. 'Silverpen', writing in the August 1847 edition of *Howetts Journal*, tells of a week on the rivers of Norfolk enjoyed in 1840 in a lateen rigged cutter. Wherries also, by this time, had been fitted out for pleasure cruising, though it was not until 1871 that the first book appeared detailing a sailing holiday so taken.

It may be difficult for us today to visualise this area, which we know so well, as wild and unspoilt, teeming with wildlife and inhabited mainly by the marshman and the wherryman. In the early decades of the 19th century, it was the naturalist rather than the holiday maker who was attracted to, and wrote about, what was to be found in the district that we know as the Broads. 1845 saw Charles Muskett publish *Observations on the Fauna of Norfolk and more particularly on the District of the Broads* written by the Rev Richard Lubbock, rector of Eccles. This slim 156 page volume, bound in green cloth, included a map of the district of the Broads as well as two etchings of pipes from the decoy at Ranworth. Henry Stacy published a second edition in 1848, and an expanded new edition, amounting to 236 pages plus a 36 page introduction, was published by Jarrold & Sons in 1879.

Lubbock had died in 1876 and it was with the encouragement of his widow, together with the loan of much manuscript material, that Thomas Southwell, a fellow naturalist, came to expand on the original volume. This new edition also included a biographical memoir of the late Richard Lubbock written by Henry Stevenson who, like Southwell, was a member of the British Ornithologists' Union. This memoir had previously appeared in the *Transactions of the Norfolk and Norwich Naturalists Society* and was reprinted with their permission. In his introduction, Thomas Southwell lamented that: 'the changes in the past thirty years (since publication of the first edition) have been greater than during any like period in the history of our Island. Railways, steam draining mills and improved cultivation have changed the quaking bogs, where once the Gull placed her procreant cradle, into green pastures where herds feed in safety; the wavy swell of the soughing reeds has given place to the bending ears of golden corn; and the boom of the Bittern, the scream of the Godwit, and the graceful flight of the

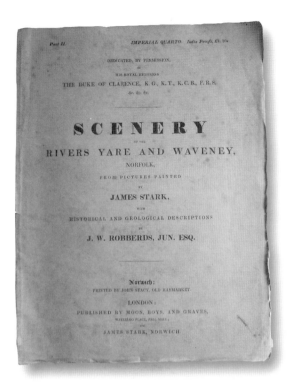

Scenery of the Rivers of Norfolk – comprising the Yare, the Waveney, and the Bure. Part 2 of 4 – issued before 'the Bure' was added to the title.

glancing Tern, are sounds and sights altogether in the past'.

In 1866 Henry Stevenson completed the first volume of his ***Birds of Norfolk*** and a second volume followed in 1870. Stevenson made much reference to sightings of birds in the Broads and included essays within the text as well as an introduction to the district in volume one. Illustrations included two fine tinted lithographs of Surlingham Broad and Breydon Water. Following Stevenson's death in 1888, Thomas Southwell undertook a third volume which was published in 1890.

By the mid 1800s much had been written by Samuel Woodward and others on the subject of the geology of Norfolk. J W Robberds, junior had completed his ***Geological and Historical Observations of the Eastern Vallies of Norfolk*** by 1826 and he also contributed the text for ***Scenery of the Rivers of Norfolk comprising the Yare, the Waveney, and the Bure*** which was finally completed by 1834. This magnificent work included twenty-four full-page and twelve vignette copper engravings from paintings by the Norwich School artist James Stark. It was originally published in four parts and intended only to include the rivers Yare and Waveney, however, in an address to subscribers in 1831 (tipped into Part Three), it was announced: 'that in order to render this Publication as complete as possible, it has been deemed advisable to include the Scenery of the River Bure, the three rivers having one common outlet to the sea'. There were 398 named subscribers* including the King, members of the nobility, gentry of the county including seven Gurneys, and additionally Norwich School contemporaries of Stark such as John Sell Cotman, two Cromes, David Hodgson, Robert Ladbrooke and Joseph Stannard. Subscribers would generally have had their parts bound into one quarto volume in a style to suit their library. There were also sixty-five large paper copies, a handful of which would have been bound to include the plates in two states – that is the finished state and an earlier 'intermediate' state.

One other early volume, dating from 1830 and in part relating to the district, should be mentioned, that being ***Picturesque Views of all the Bridges belonging to the County***

Acle Bridge, from a series of 84 lithographs by Francis Stone.

of Norfolk in a Series of 84 Prints in Lithography by Francis Stone, surveyor of bridges to the County Council. This was also published in four parts and in total comprised the title page and eighty-four full page oblong uncoloured lithographs taken from drawings by David Hodgson; there was no text. Several of the bridges in broadland were illustrated showing river activity with wherry traffic in evidence. This work is of particular value in that it illustrates many bridges subsequently replaced.

* It was common in the 18th and early decades of the 19th century for topographical works containing many (expensive) engravings to be sold by prior subscription and in parts. This allowed the cost for the subscriber to be spread over a number of years, and of course helped finance the venture for the author or publisher. The work would often include a list of those that had so subscribed; when finally completed and distributed the purchaser would then have the parts bound up by his binder in a style to suit his library. Individual parts of many of these works are still seen from time to time today, sometimes lacking their engravings which would have been removed for framing. Often these parts contained important bibliographical information which would subsequently be lost when bound. Other important Norfolk topographical works originally issued in parts included Ladbrookes Churches and both Blomefields and Armstrongs Histories of Norfolk.

INTO THE 1870s

In 1865 Chapman and Hall published two volumes of travel excursions by Walter White. Entitled ***Eastern England from the Thames to the Humber***, they relate to excursions or trips taken by the author within parts of Norfolk, Suffolk, Essex and Lincolnshire. Completed a year or two before publication, volume one devotes fifty pages to a cruise by White on *The Adelaide* which commenced at Coltishall and eventually ended up at Great Yarmouth. Much description of the scenery and life along the way was included which makes this a most readable volume and perhaps the earliest guidebook with any real human detail of the broadland district. Volume two, outlining his meanderings about Suffolk a year later, sees White meet up with *The Adelaide* at Oulton Broad and he also sails on the Waveney to Beccles and then further.

Wilkie Collins was an acclaimed 19th century novelist and sailing was a favourite pastime which he undertook to relieve his 'rheumatic gout'. The summer of 1864 saw him on a sailing expedition off the Norfolk coast when he took the opportunity to explore part of the Norfolk Broads, and in particular the area around Horsey. Part of his latest novel ***Armadale***, published in two volumes in 1866 but previously serialised in the *Cornhill* magazine, was set in this area of the Broads which undoubtably would then have been fresh in his mind:

"Perhaps you may have heard of the Norfolk Broads, sir? What they call lakes in other parts of England, they call Broads here. The Broads are quite numerous; I think they would repay a visit.... Mostly shallow, sir, with rivers running between them. Beautiful; solitary.... Parties sometimes visit them, sir – pleasure-parties in boats. It's quite a little network of lakes, or, perhaps – yes, perhaps more correctly, pools."

It would appear that Wilkie Collins was the first novelist to base a story around this district.

The first description in book form of a holiday on the Broads was not long in following and C A Campling, in August 1871, with ***The Log of the Stranger, a Cruise on the Broads of Norfolk*** relates how he as the Steward joined Fred Burtsall (Captain), Harry Campling (Mate) and Nelson Burtsall (Purser) on *The Stranger*, a cutter-rigged yacht, for a trip from Great Yarmouth which eventually ended at Horning. The Log of the Stranger sets the style that subsequent volumes followed – setting the scene, introducing the crew, the exploits of the inexperienced sailors, the food eaten and drink imbibed, and the scenery that unfolded, all told in a jocular style. One additional member of the crew, in this case Tungate described as Mariner and 'Reliable Man', was the hired hand who, though knowing his place, kept everybody in some form of order and actually knew how and where to sail. The first paragraph of the preface in the slim

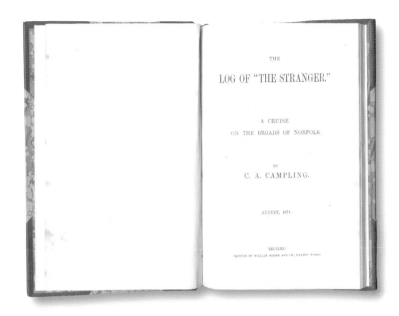

Title page of the Log of the Stranger.

58 page volume states: 'The success achieved and the amusement afforded by a previous log has induced me to comply with the wishes of the crew, to put the present log into form. I trust it will be found a pleasant record of a happy time'.

The previous log so referred probably relates to an earlier trip which was not published until 1872 and titled **The Log of a Trip Taken in 1867 on the Rivers and Broads of Norfolk**.

The 1870s also saw the first writings from George Christopher Davies who was immortalised in his obituary as 'The Man who found the Broads'. Born of Welsh parents, and following a grammar school education, he served articles and qualified as a solicitor in 1871. By chance he happened to read an article in *The Field* by Greville F (Barnes) descriptive of the Norfolk Broads. Attracted by the possibilities as 'a water vagabond' and procuring a legal journal he found an advertisement for a vacancy as a managing clerk in the practice of Abel Tillett in Norwich. This he successfully applied for, took up lodgings in the city, and found a fascination for the Broads' district which lasted throughout his life. His initial spell in Norwich only lasted until the following year when he took up a position with a large firm of solicitors in Newcastle-on-Tyne and was able to specialise in the commercial side of law. In 1874 he married Louisa Alice Cooper, the daughter of a Norwich solicitor, and they had two children whilst living in Newcastle. The return to Norwich, which became permanent, took place in 1879 when he set up in practice with his father-in-law at 58 London Street. Christopher Davies' first book **Mountain, Meadow and Mere** was published in 1873 and consisted of natural history sketches or chapters, some of which related to Norfolk and the Broads. His first book specifically based on the Broads was published by

Frederick Warne & Co in 1876 whilst he was still practising law in Newcastle. This was the magnificent *The Swan and her Crew*, the story of Frank, Jimmy and Dick, and their adventures as naturalists and sportsmen. In today's world of health and safety, their 'Boys Own' style adventures seem almost unbelievable; the *Swan* was the sailing boat built by the boys – chapter one tells of the felling of a larch tree, Frank's chosen present from his father for his birthday (it seems unclear whether the present was the tree or the actual felling!). Chapter five describes and illustrates the boys' endeavours in constructing the *Swan* from this tree, and there-on their adventures – sailing, fishing, birding, the flora and fauna and so forth – to the conclusion of the book in chapter forty-one.

The Swan and her Crew was Davies' seventh published book and clearly to date the most successful. It quickly ran to several editions and such was the response that a twenty-four page postscript was added to the fourth in which Davies wrote: "Of course I was greatly pleased with the wide interest taken in the adventures of the *Swan* and her crew on the broads and rivers of Norfolk. I received a great many letters asking for further details, and some readers wished to make a craft like the *Swan*. Now just the same fun can be extracted out of a cruise in a craft of normal build; and such a cruise is not at all expensive.

"Shortly after writing the 'Swan', I determined to take another look at the 'Broads', for writing about them had whetted my appetite for their beauties. I accordingly undertook a cruise, and I thought that this recital of it might be welcome to those who had read the 'Swan', and who might wish to take a similar cruise."

This cruise, as related in the postscript, was on the *Queen of the Bure* which ended, as it had started, at Coltishall.

"It will not be amiss to give some information as to the cost of such a cruise. The hire of our yacht was two pounds, three shillings a week, and the man's wages were twenty-two shillings and sixpence a week.... and of course you have to find the man with provisions."

By the early 1890s 'The Swan' had reached a seventh edition; Jarrolds took over from Warnes and republished in the early 1920s with the last edition being published by Methuen in 1932, having been revised by his son Hugh Davies. In many ways *The Swan and her Crew* was a pivotal book. It is said that Arthur Ransome was inspired on reading it to write **Swallow and Amazons*, but also that holiday cruise on the *Queen of the Bure* may well have set the course for Davies to write his famous *Handbook to the Rivers and Broads of Norfolk and Suffolk*.

* Swallow and Amazons of course was set in the Lakes, however, Ransome wrote two later books based on the Broads: Coot Club and The Big Six.

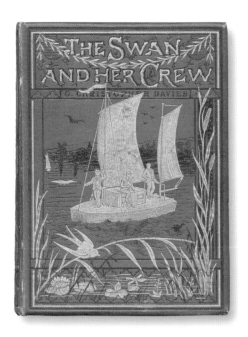

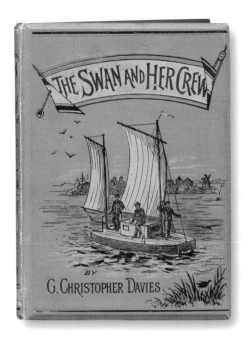

*The Swan and Her Crew by
G Christopher Davies. 1st edition.*

*The Swan and Her Crew by
G Christopher Davies. New edition.*

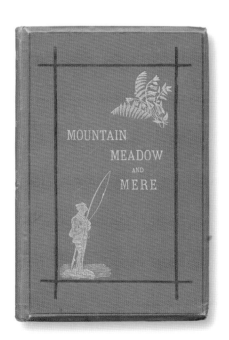

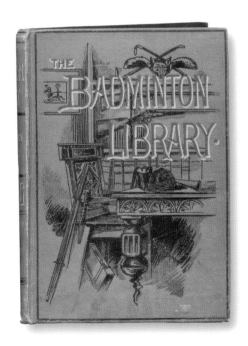

*Mountain Meadow and Mere by
G Christopher Davies.*

The Badminton Library.

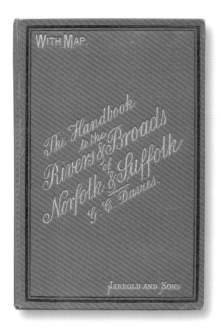

Handbook to the Rivers & Broads of Norfolk & Suffolk. 1st edition 1882.

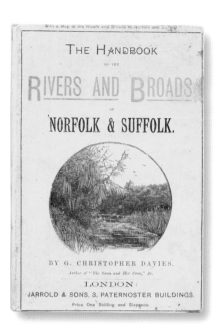

Handbook to the Rivers and Broads of Norfolk & Suffolk. 7th edition.

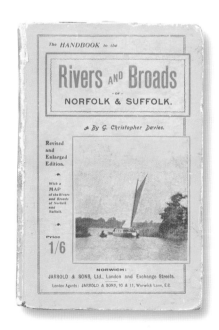

Handbook to the Rivers and Broads of Norfolk & Suffolk. 41st edition.

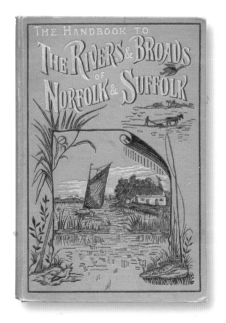

Handbook to the Rivers & Broads of Norfolk & Suffolk. 18th edition.

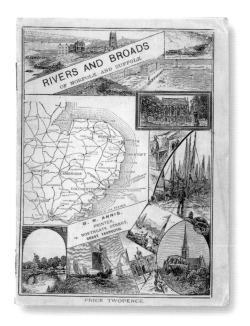

*Rivers and Broads of Norfolk
and Suffolk. Circa 1890.*

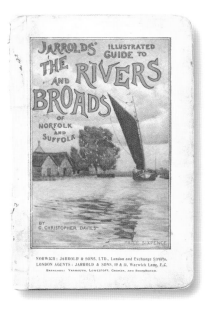

*Rivers and Broads of Norfolk
and Suffolk. 44th edition.*

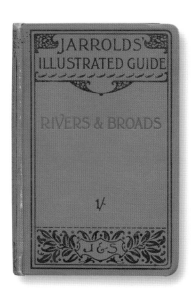

*Jarrolds' Illustrated Guide,
Rivers & Broads. 36th edition.*

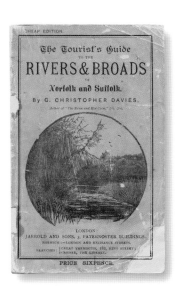

*The Tourist's Guide to
Rivers & Broads.
21st edition.*

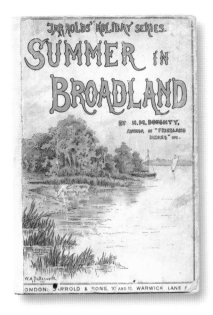

Summer in Broadland. 1890.
Bettesworth illustrated cover.

Summer in Broadland.
Title page dated 1889, but is later.

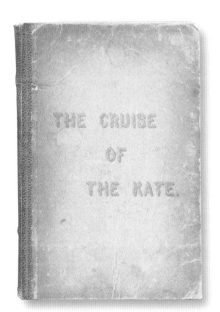

The Cruise of the Kate.

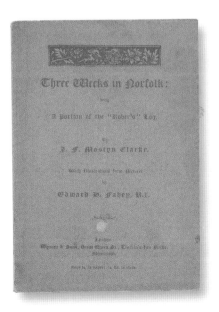

Three Weeks in Norfolk.
Thin card bound edition.

THE MAN WHO FOUND THE BROADS

*T**he Handbook to the Rivers and Broads of Norfolk and Suffolk*** by George Christopher Davies was published by Jarrold & Sons in 1882 and was almost continually in print until the early 1930s when the fiftieth and last edition, illustrated by the well known broadland artist Walter Leslie Rackham, was released. The first edition, with the preface dated February 1882, was a slim 108 page volume with just a few local adverts to the front and rear, these being mainly for accommodation and fisheries. The only boat hirer who advertised was John Loynes who took a full page and described himself as 'John Loynes, Boat Builder, Elm Hill, Norwich'. He advertised hire terms from £1/10s per week without attendance and from £3/3s with, and announced that some boats are stationed at Wroxham with others obtainable from Elm Hill in Norwich. It was not until 1887, with the ninth revised and enlarged edition, that the text was expanded to 173 pages and clearly more tradesmen thought it beneficial to advertise. John Loynes was joined by the Press Brothers from North Walsham who stated that the wherry-yachts *Bertha*, *Elsie*, *Kate*, *Dilligent*, and *Lucy* 'Are fitted with every Convenience for the Enjoyment of Parties wishing to Visit the Rivers and Broads of Norfolk'. Also J Hart & Son of Thorpe Village advertised having on hand for hire a good selection of yachts and boats suitable for cruising about the Norfolk waters. Subsequent revisions and enlargements (11th revision of 1888, and 15th revised and enlarged 1890) were stated on the title pages but the format and page count remained identical to that of 1887 edition until, with the twenty-ninth edition of 1899, additional information increased the number of pages to just over 200. The addition of details of the wild birds protection acts 1880–1896, seen from about the forty-first edition (railway advert dated this edition to 1906), pushed the page count to 206, and this remained constant to the forty-fifth and last edition noted before the Rackham illustrated edition, mentioned above.

George Christopher Davies

Apart from the text, it appears that Jarrolds applied little conformity as far as the editions and adverts were concerned. There were three main bindings throughout the series, two in cloth (one being the standard Jarrolds' 'Holiday Series' format which was also used for books by other authors) and one in yellow card boards which were much prone to wear. It is quite possible that some edition numbers were missed out, and also adverts sometimes differed in volumes of the same edition. Apart from revision dates, I have never seen an actual publication date on any title page and volumes can only generally be dated from railway adverts and inscriptions. To further complicate matters, Davies' text was utilised by Jarrolds in other titles: ***Jarrolds' Illustrated Guide to the Rivers and Broads of Norfolk and Suffolk*** was a publication in illustrated card boards with rounded corners and tended to be later numbered editions, and ***The Tourists' Guide to the Rivers and Broads of Norfolk & Suffolk***, whilst still sharing Davies' text, were much slighter smaller volumes in various cloth and thin card/paper bindings. The earliest of these that I have seen is in red cloth with rounded corners and contains an Eastern & Midlands Railway advert dated July 1883; others noted have been marked as twenty-first and thirty-sixth editions. One other title should also be mentioned, this being ***Rivers and Broads of Norfolk and Suffolk***. These were 24 page, paper- or thin card-covered guidebooks also based on Davies' writings. The contents of the earliest, from the 1880s, are very much in the style of the 'Handbook', but later ones from about the 1920s indicate on the cover that they are by G Christopher Davies but, on the title page, compiled by Lt-Col R F Lush (some issues omit this but indicate RFL on page 24).

Without any doubt 'The Handbook' was a huge commercial success for Jarrolds, however, it was not the book for which Davies wished to be remembered. He wrote in the preface to the early editions: "I find that an intention of mine to some day write a book on the Broads has got wind, and while I am flattered at the enquiries I constantly receive as to the time of its appearance, I must confess that at present the intention has not matured into action, and I have got no further than the note-taking."

Davies goes on to say that he found a reluctance from those in the know to pass on information, and that there was much he needed to learn about the eel-fishers and wherrymen and their lives and manners, pursuits, customs and traditions. He also complained that he only had time to write at night and of that he was less fond than previously: " I hope that this little book will meet the need which my publishers believe to exist, and for myself I trust that it may elicit for me some practical encouragement – in the shape of proffered information on the lines I have indicated – to the realization of my more ambitious intention."

That 'more ambitious intention' came to fulfilment the following year when William Blackwood and Sons published ***Norfolk Broads and Rivers or the Water-Ways, Lagoons, and Decoys of East Anglia***. This was an entirely more substantial work than that commissioned in 1882 by Jarrolds. It ran to 290 pages with forty chapters of topography, flora and fauna, social history and geography, as well as four relating to 'Cruises of the *Coya*' (Davies' own yacht) and eight pages relating to 'a merry cruise on the Ant and Thurne'. This substantially bound volume was published in light brown

Rockland Broad. Photogravure from the 1883 1st edition of Norfolk Broads and Rivers or the Waterways, Lagoons, and Decoys of East Anglia by G C Davies.

cloth (a slightly cheaper green cloth version has also been noted) with gilt lettering to the spine and a yachting scene, also in gilt, to the top board. It also contained twelve splendid full page photogravure illustrations etched by Annans, the famous Glaswegian firm who were the specialists in this form of photographic reproduction. All bar one were taken by Davies who prided himself on his photographic capabilities, and whose work is still commonly found today in collections and at auction. In the preface it stated that some of the chapters had previously appeared in *Blackwood's Magazine* with parts of others having also been printed in various other publications such as *The Field*, *East Anglian Handbook*, *Gentleman's Magazine* and *The Art Journal*. In his preface, Davies also writes: "....there is an engrossing charm in the lakes and rivers of East Anglia. No one knows better than the Author how strong this feeling is, and no one perhaps has been guilty of writing so much on the subject. This book, however, is positively his last appearance in the field of descriptive writing anent the Broads."

Though expensive to produce, the book must have been a success as in 1884 a second or 'new edition' was published. Bound in a similar though slightly smaller and cheaper brown cloth, this new edition ran to 328 pages plus at the rear a book catalogue advertising Blackwood's publications. The expensive photogravure plates were dispensed with, being replaced with seven cheaper wood-engraved views. No further editions were published, however, Davies' yearning to write an authorative and informative book about the Broads appeared to have been satisfied.

With publication of the 'Handbook' in 1882, the collaboration of Davies with Jarrolds was not quite finished as far as the Broads were concerned. In 1883 Jarrold &

Sons published two series of photo-engravings by Annan taken from Davies' photographs. There were twenty-four loose photogravures, measuring 6" x 4", in each set, either printed directly onto folio-sized paper or onto India paper which was then pasted to the folio-sized backing. Each plate was captioned with a tiny titled label affixed to the lower corner of the white surrounding mount. ***The Scenery of the Broads and Rivers of Norfolk and Suffolk*** was published as a first series and a second series, with the plates loosely laid within folders, the top board of which was printed with the title, photographer, publisher and the price of one guinea. Many sets have now been split up and individual plates are commonly seen. Towards the end of the decade, Jarrold & Sons re-issued this work, this time as one set of all forty-eight photogravures bound in an oblong volume with a page of brief descriptive text preceding each illustration. Bound sets are comparatively rare so it is probable that the re-issue was not an overwhelming commercial success.

George Christopher Davies wrote many other books, some about fishing which only touch on the Broads, and others, both fiction and non fiction, which do not come within the compass of this bibliography at all. He was also a prolific writer of articles, many of which of course were about fishing, sailing and tourism in this district. A second volume, and years of research, would be required to do justice to this aspect of ephemeral broadland literature. In closing this chapter, Davies' contribution to two volumes of ***The Badminton Library*** should be mentioned. The volume ***Fishing*** in this series edited by H Cholmondeley-Pennell was published in two parts, the second of which was subtitled 'Pike and other Coarse Fish' and included a 24 page chapter by Davies on 'Norfolk Broad and River Fishing'. Also in the series, the volume entitled ***Yachting*** also came out in two volumes with Davies contributing 'Yachting on the Norfolk Broads' on 37 pages in volume two. Volumes of the Badminton Library, in their distinctive decorated brown boards, were generally published during the 1880s and 1890s.

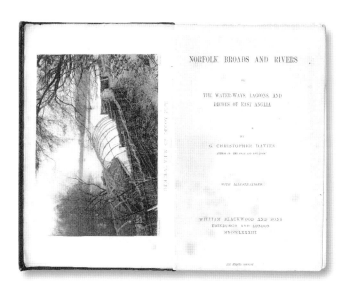

Norfolk Broads and Rivers by G Christopher Davies. 1st edition, 1883.

THROUGH THE 1880s

George Christopher Davies, without question, composed by far the most successful broadland guidebook, however, it did not stop others from attempting to emulate his success. As well, tourism inevitably grew and as the professional classes took to these waters some felt inclined to record their adventures and have their writings privately printed in small editions, perhaps for sale to family and friends left at home.

The only guide to be published contemporarily with 'the Handbook' was *The Broads and Rivers of Norfolk with chart and map showing the various points of interest, railway lines and stations, &c.* This slim 51 page volume comprised text that had previously appeared in the *Norwich Argus* and was published by P Soman based in St Giles, Norwich. It included a folding map showing the rivers, broads and railway lines, local adverts to the rear (Loynes took a half page) and a preface announcing 'a desire to make the Broads and Rivers of Norfolk known beyond the circle of the County.' The only indication as to compiler was the initials 'W F', and there was a date June 1882 at the close of the preface. Clearly it did not rival its Jarrolds' near name-sake, and the text was reprinted in the 1883 edition of the *East Anglian Handbook*. Both the *Argus* and the *East Anglian Handbook* (which appeared annually for many years and was fertile ground for broadland articles written by well known authorities) were from the Soman stable of publications.

1883 saw the private printing of *A Week on the Broads* by R M N, a 90 page lithographically-printed manuscript account of a sailing holiday taken in that year. A copy surfaced at auction just over ten years ago and it is not known how many copies were printed. In all probability it was produced for the sole benefit of family and friends.

November 1886 saw the printing of *The Cruise of the Kate a Narrative of a very merry Wherry Expedition through the Rivers & Broads of Norfolk & Suffolk by One of the Crew* (E M Harvey – the 'Scribe'). Printed in Stamford, from whence most of the twelve crew members originated, it was the most comprehensive and professionally written of the 'Holidays on the Broads' genre. 137 pages long, it also included a map of 'our route' and the all male crew were known by nickname with their real names indicated by their initials. The short preface announced: "Our apology for appearing in print is not that the places we visited are unknown to our friends, but that they have been so persistent in their enquiries as to how we spent the twelve days of absence from the civilised world." One member of that crew – C S H B or 'Chitimaru' – was Cloudesley Brereton who contributed an article to the 1936 edition of the *Norfolk Annual* entitled 'Early Memories of the Broads'. Inspired by reading 'Swan and her

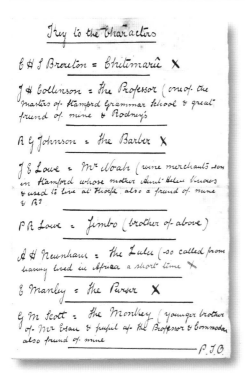

Manuscript details of the crew of The Kate.

Crew' as a young man, he tells of how for several years from 1882 he spent holidays sailing on the Broads, and how in 1886 he and eleven others hired a wherry with a piano, described as the most vocal of the party. "They were mostly Cambridge men, one of whom wrote a book called *The Cruise of the Kate*, which sold quite well."

1886 seems to have been a popular year for writing about trips taken on these waters; ***Three Weeks in Norfolk being a Portion of the 'Rover's' Log*** was completed in November and printed by Wyman & Sons the following year. Written by J F Mostyn Clarke and attractively illustrated from pictures by Edward Fahey RE, it tells of a holiday, which started from Yarmouth, taken by the writer and his artist friend on the yacht *Rover*.

In the preface Mostyn Clarke writes: "In writing down the following more or less detailed account of a short holiday, spent last year in Norfolk, I have been led by a wish to preserve some faithful record of our adventure in gratitude for the many pleasant days enjoyed with my friend on board his yacht. Never having visited either Norfolk or Suffolk, I gladly availed myself of an invitation that would enable me to know my friend better, and more of the workaday life on one whose labours rank high in the Art World. During the short period I was with him – but a fraction of his expedition – my friend H——— was engaged upon pictures intended for exhibition in London."

In the third paragraph from page one he states: "How fresh and cool after the dust and heat of London was the light sea-breeze; how refreshing the sight of sparkling, dancing water, after the dull monotony of endless streets! What relief to throw aside the stereotyped costume of Pall Mall and Regent street for the simple and easy garments of a yachting holiday!"

A few days were spent moored within sight of Wroxham bridge and following exploration of the village it was found as 'a pleasant and simple country hamlet, inconsiderable in extent, and with nothing to lead one to describe it at length'.

The *Rover* was skippered by a local whose conduct left much to be desired and several pages are devoted to the altercations leading to our visitors' abandonment. A replacement, Bob, unfortunately did not prove any more successful becoming very drunk and abusive. Perhaps it was a case of classes not mixing in such an intimate setting! *Three Weeks in Norfolk* was published at 1s in printed brown-paper covers and at 1s 6d in cloth; copies can be deemed very scarce and are infrequently seen.

In very much the same style *Journal of a short Cruise on the Rivers and Broads of Norfolk and Suffolk* was printed in 1889 for 'private circulation' by Richard Clay & Sons. The writer was Charles Edward Brennan, a dentist who lived in Norwich, and he hired the ten-ton yacht *The Emily* and wrote about his holiday, accompanied by brothers Arthur, Harold and William Beard, which commenced from Thorpe and ended at Oulton Broad, with the train back to Norwich. This slim 64 page book is very much in the style of others – their daily adventures (would this seem very tame today?), where they sailed, food and drink, locals etc. The only copy that I have seen is in the ownership of a direct descendant of the family and is simply bound in a dark full-leather binding with gilt tooling. It is likely that the print run was very small and mainly for distribution to family and friends.

I have tried to avoid including the many articles published in magazines, with Christopher Davies himself having penned probably more than twenty. Sometimes, however, these were reprinted in book form, or at least as a pamphlet. Such was *The Log of the Lalage being a description of a Cruise on the Norfolk Broads*. This 40 page booklet, bound in printed paper wrappers with a railway advert dated 1891, had previously appeared in the August and September 1889 issues of *Tinsley's* magazine (new series) and is rare in either form.

The 1880s also saw writings by Ernest Suffling, Harry Brittain and Walter Rye, and these I have recorded in subsequent chapters. Those apart, the publication in 1889 of *Summer in Broadland: Gipsying in East Anglian Waters* by The Author of 'Friesland Meres' &c (Henry Montagu Doughty) saw the most commercial success. Published by Jarrold & Sons in their 'Holiday' series, it tells in its 136 pages the story of a wherry trip by the author, his son, two daughters, James the cook and steward, and Sam the only member of the crew. The party started off by sailing from Aylsham to Coltishall and then throughout the northern and southern river systems, to Bungay and then back again, and ending the trip at Wroxham via Somerton and Horsey. Much trouble was encountered with Ludham bridge; with their first approach they literally scraped through but a return journey, with the water level high, necessitated co-operation from a trading wherry: "We bargained with the master to load upon the *Gipsy* weight enough to put her down six inches. Sacks were hoisted out of the trader's hold, and the master, his mate, and Sam heaped our deck with them – fore-deck, plank-ways, cock-pit, were all cumbered. Now gently, cautiously, we approach the arch, to be repelled with grating harsh denial. A line of more sacks is laid along the cabin-top, beside the lowered mast. Another and a bolder offer is successful. We have fought for, and have won our freedom."

Summer in Broadland ran to at least six editions, but as seen previously with Jarrold's publications, the edition and dating can be confusing. The sixth edition apparently is dated 1897, however earlier editions dated 1890 also contain railway adverts with the date of 1897! Various bindings have been noted, the standard cloth and gilt 'Holiday Series' binding is commonly seen and there is a later and cheaper cloth binding in a similar style but without the gilt. W A Bettesworth provided artwork for a coloured printed scene on a card bound version and other designs have also been noted.

Doughty wrote two other books relating his wherry trips: *Friesland Meres and Through the Netherlands the Voyage of a Family in a Norfolk Wherry* was published at about the same time as *Summer in Broadland*, with *Our Wherry in Wendish Lands* a year or two later. Both books tell of the family's adventures in the *Gipsy*. Henry Montagu Doughty clearly came from wealthy stock as among the crew on both trips was his butler who 'played the parts of cook and steward'. In fact, being the eldest son, he had inherited several houses and estates following the death of his father at the relatively early age of 52. These were spread over various parishes in Suffolk and included Theberton Hall, the family seat. His younger brother was the noted explorer and travel writer Charles Montagu Doughty.

The final year of the decade saw Cassell & Company publish two large volumes entitled *Rivers of Great Britain, Descriptive, Historical, Pictorial*. These were subtitled *Rivers of the East Coast* and, like many other similar works published up to the 1930s by major publishing houses, were initially sold by subscription. The waters of broadland were not described until the final chapter of the second volume where W Senior wrote about the rivers of East Anglia including the Waveney, Bure and Yare, as well as the Broads generally. Included with the text was a fine large full-page etching entitled 'On Wroxham Broad'. This plate, as well as the other eleven etchings that accompany this work, was only to be found in the special subscribers edition and is lacking in the ordinary edition which is more commonly seen and was on general sale in bookshops.

Two other books of Broads' interest and published in the closing years of the decade should also be mentioned. *By Leafy Ways* written by F A Knight comprises a series of 'Brief Studies from the Book of Nature'. From these, 'By Quiet Waters' with its accompanying photogravure, is an essay about the Broads.

Afloat on the Norfolk Broads by Geo C Haite FLS comprised 12 pages of verse on thin card, interspersed with chromolithographic views of broadland scenes from drawings by the author. This style of 'presentation' or gift booklet was widely sold in the closing years of the nineteenth century and was generally printed in Germany, as was this title. It came with an accompanying printed envelope in identical design and marked 'With best wishes From ____'. These envelopes have seldom survived.

Idylls of the Norfolk Broads, by P H Emerson Edition limited to 100 copies. (Note: Idyls is spelt with a double 'l' to the cover, but with a single 'l' to the text, which is the form Emerson generally adhered to.)

A decorative portfolio with a collection of twelve atmospheric loose photogravures of varying sizes, together with a title page.

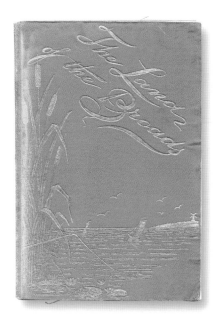

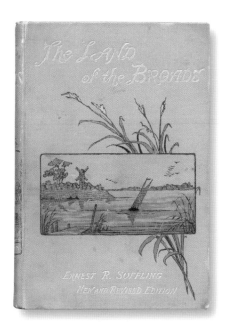

*The Land of the Broads.
1st non-illustrated edition.*

*The Land of the Broads.
'Standard' illustrated boards.*

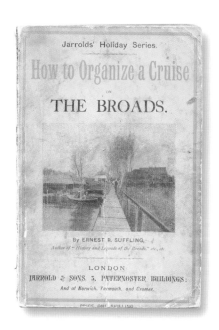

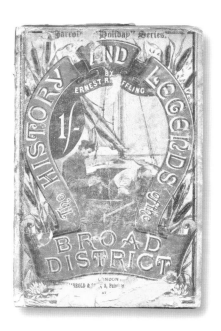

*How to Organize a Cruise on the
Broads, by Ernest Suffling.
Later edition.*

*The History and Legends of the
Broad District. Later edition.*

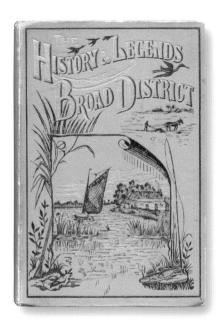

History & Legends of the Broad
District by Ernest Suffling.

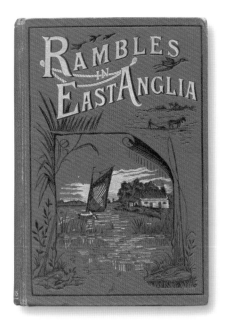

Rambles in East Anglia
by Harry Brittain.

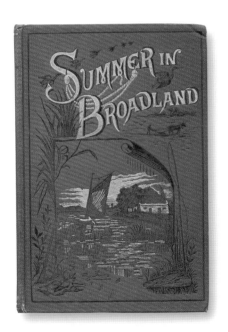

Summer in Broadland
by H M Doughty.

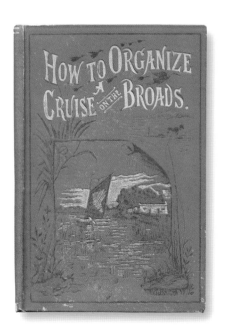

How to Organize a Cruise on the
Broads by Ernest Suffling.

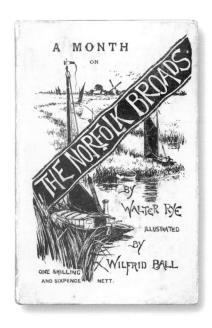

A Month on the Norfolk Broads, by Walter Rye.

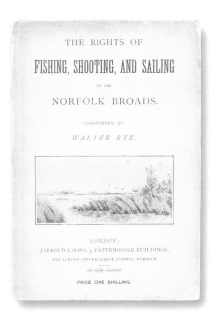

The Rights of Fishing, Shooting, and Sailing on the Norfolk Broads.

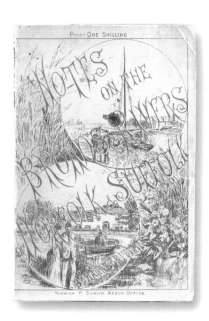

Notes on the Broads & Rivers of Norfolk & Suffolk by Harry Brittain.

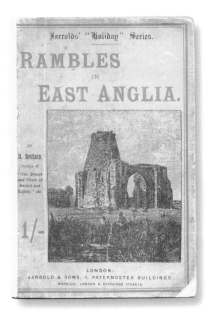

Rambles in East Anglia by Harry Brittain.

ERNEST R SUFFLING

There was one other descriptive guidebook of the Broads which rivalled that compiled by Christopher Davies; this was ***The Land of the Broads, a Practical and Illustrated Guide to the Broads of Norfolk & Suffolk*** by Ernest R Suffling. Unlike Davies, Suffling did claim to be a Norfolk man and a native of the Broad's district; but he lived in London when he wrote this popular guide. Also, like Davies, Suffling wrote extensively on all sorts of other subjects including boys adventure novels (including one based on the Broads and described in a subsequent chapter), church related volumes, a guidebook to Epping and in 1910, whilst living at 'The Turet Hasbro', a history and guide to Happisburgh which was published by subscription.

The first edition of the *Land of the Broads* was published in 1885 by Upcott Gill in a slim red cloth and gilt 80 page volume with a map but no illustrations. It was then entitled ***The Land of the Broads, a practical Guide for Yachtsmen, Anglers, Tourists, and other Pleasure-Seekers on the Broads and Rivers of Norfolk and Suffolk***. An undated (railway ad. May 1887) thin card bound version soon followed, but which now had six full-page broadland scenes in addition to the map. Upcott Gill was renowned for the attractive illustrated covers to their publications and this volume did not disappoint having superb chromolitho boards illustrating a pike and a bittern amongst reeds*. Both volumes are scarce, particularly the card bound version, so were presumably published in relatively small numbers. It seems, however, that sales were sufficiently buoyant that it encouraged the publisher to commission Suffling to write an expanded 318 page 'Illustrated' second edition. This was published also in May 1887 and the title was suffixed with '*A Practical and Illustrated Guide to the Extensive but little-known District of the Broads of Norfolk and Suffolk. Written for the use of all who take an interest in one of the Quaintest and most Old-World parts of England, either from an Archaeological, Historical, Picturesque, or Sporting point of view.*'

Publication of the title passed to Benjamin Perry of Stratford in Essex (publishers to the Great Eastern Railway) by 1892 and, apart from their name, the edition was virtually identical and still referred to as the second edition. Clearly the Broads was no longer the 'little-known District' that it had previously been as the advertising pages of this edition gave space to more than forty boat hirers!

Easter 1895 saw a 'Re-Written and Illustrated Edition' and Suffling in his preface to this, the seventh, edition stated: "Ten years has witnessed a great change in the Land of the Broads, for where, less than a decade ago the district was known to but few, it is now annually visited and enjoyed by thousands.... ....The demand for this volume has been so great that it was found necessary (in these up-to-date times) that it should undergo revision, so many changes having taken place since it was written."

The boat hire adverts to the rear of the text were further expanded, and also included a page offering yachts and a wherry by Suffling himself from his London address. It is assumed that this the seventh, commonest and last edition, remained in print for some considerable time. However, despite having handled many copies I must say that I have yet to note any stated edition between the second and seventh.

Ernest Suffling in his preface to the second edition of ***The Land of the Broads*** stated: "By letting my pen run free with anecdotes, songs of the fens, local tales, and traditions, I might have made the present volume a very substantial tome, but have refrained from doing so, as these things, although extremely interesting, are not, perhaps, that my worthy publisher desires – 'a practical guide only'."

By courtesy of Jarrold & Sons in their 'Holiday Series', Ernest Suffling was now able to allow his pen to run more freely, writing two undated books which were both published in this series in about 1891. In ***The History & Legends of the Broad District*** Suffling writes: "It has been my endeavour, while writing and compiling the following pages, to 'steer clear' of what has already been written in the Guide Books, and to give the general reader and tourist a further insight into matters connected with the district, which only one who is a native of the place can give with any degree of confidence and correctness."

This 217 page book was published in the Jarrolds' standard cloth-and-gilt binding as well as in card boards with both a Bettesworth illustrated and a photographically-illustrated version. Internally all the editions appear identical.

The second volume he completed was ***How to Organise a Cruise on the Broads***. Again published by Jarrold & Sons in their 'Holiday Series' and bound both in cloth-and-gilt as well as in card boards with again both Bettesworth and photographically illustrated cover versions, this perhaps had a longer shelf life than ***History and Legends*** with different editions indicated on the title page. Apart from the first, I have noted that a third edition dated from 1897, and a revised and enlarged fourth from 1909 with a fifth edition following. In his introduction, Suffling states: "The book then, simply aims at being a help in the arrangement and carrying out of any contemplated cruise which the reader, being a stranger to these waters, thinks he would like to undertake. The experience herein contained may be taken as the practical knowledge gained by the writer on these waters during the past twenty-five years."

* This book is illustrated on the front cover with two other books written by Ernest Suffling.

HARRY BRITTAIN
AND WALTER RYE

Harry Brittain was by profession a banker and spent his career with Barclays Bank rising to become the manager of the St Stephens branch in Norwich. He also resided there, at Bank House, which I assume was 'over the bank', until his retirement in the early part of the twentieth century when he moved to the Newmarket Road area of the city. As a young bank clerk his interest in the rivers and broads was not 'wetted' until, in the spring of 1882, he became the owner of a three-ton cutter, the *Nobby*: "At the end of the season I had become so infatuated with yachting that I determined to try a larger craft, and purchased the *Buttercup*, 8 tons."

This was of course at the same time that Christopher Davies' famous guidebook came to be published and tourism tentatively was sprouting 'green shoots'. As with so many both before and after, Harry Brittain felt the need to write about this new world that was opening up to the professional classes – he wrote to the editor of ***The Holiday Annual*** offering his services to write 'an account of a trip on the Norfolk Broads and Rivers'. This was quickly accepted with ***The Cruise of the Buttercup*** appearing in the second issue of the 1884 edition, and with ***A Peep at the 'Broads', or a Corinthian Trip on the Bure and Thurn*** following soon after.

Further magazine articles by Brittain soon followed and ***Fourteen Days Afloat: a Cruise on the Broads and Rivers of Norfolk and Suffolk*** was serialised in 1885 in the March, April and May issues of Hunt's Yachting Magazine. These articles were also published by Hunt & Co of Edgware Road, London NW in an undated large octavo 19 page book which also contained six fine full-page albumen photographs of broadland scenes. The only copy that I have seen was handsomely bound in red cloth with the title diagonally in gilt to the top board and the initials HB beneath.

Favourable reception to his articles, and having gained more practical experience of the broads and rivers, led Brittain to undertake the compilation of a full-sized work and, in May 1887, P Soman at the Argus Office published ***Notes on the Broads and Rivers of Norfolk & Suffolk***. This 154 page book was written in a personal narrative, and was both instructive and detailed. It was clearly successful as, by the following year, the text had been enlarged with three additional chapters and a 'Second and Enlarged Edition' was published. Editions are seen both in cloth and with decorated card boards.

By 1890 the flood of books and articles about the Broads was ever increasing, and Brittain himself questioned the need for more: "Perhaps I have been as guilty as any one in persistently forcing the claims of our silent highways on public attention, but I receive many direct and pleasurable proofs that I have not written altogether in vain.

For all this, the issue of another work bearing so largely on my pet topic may be considered quite unnecessary. My reply to criticism on this point is, that my publishers do not think so, and surely they, of all men, have the best opportunity of gauging public wishes in matters of this kind."

The publishers so mentioned were Jarrold & Sons, and it seems it was they who approached Harry Brittain, then living at Blofield, with the view to him writing another book on this subject. The result, published in 1890, was *Rambles in East Anglia: or, Holiday Excursions among the Rivers and Broads*. This 150 page volume tells of the adventures and excursions of three young friends, based at Great Yarmouth, who make holiday jaunts to places of note in the district. Much time is spent on the broads and rivers, but visits to Norwich, Lowestoft, Cromer and Southwold were also undertaken. Published in the Jarrolds 'Holiday Series', this title was issued in the usual cloth gilt version as well as in at least two card versions, including one with a fine Bettesworth cover illustration. Other editions have been noted including a third with the date 1897.

Brittain was to write no further books, but his love for the Broad's district remained. Subsequent to his ownership of the *Buttercup*, he purchased the wherry *Zoe* which Walter Rye tells of in his *Songs, Stories and Sayings of Norfolk (1897)* – 'The first expensively fitted up pleasure wherry was the great unwieldy *Zoe*, of Norwich, the style of which has been followed by very many.'

The wherry Zoe.

The wherry Zoe.

Rye's book also contained the first printed bibliography of books written about the Broads. Walter Rye was one of the most remarkable characters that Norfolk and Norwich has ever seen. A prolific historian, writer and compiler of books and articles, his library, with that of the Colmans, formed the marvellous 'Colman and Rye' collection in the local studies library and which was subsequently largely destroyed by fire. He was a solicitor, businessman, the last mayor of Norwich, owned and restored the Maids Head hotel and Bacon's House in Norwich, saved the Lazar House from demolition, was an athlete of distinction and so much more which he relates in *An Autobiography of an Ancient Athlete & Antiquary (1916)*. He also purchased in 1890 the old trading wherry *Alma* which he had converted to a pleasure wherry, but previously in 1885 had bought the *Lotus* which he described as 'an old round-topped boat with a short jib'. Rye relates that its wide berths and comfortable cabin took his fancy and he was able to purchase it fairly cheaply. He then had it cleaned and, finding that it was actually mahogany built, had it restored to something like its original state. The story by Walter Rye, published in 1887 by Simpkin, Marshall and Co, of the Lotus' first cruise is told in the book *A Month on the Norfolk Broads on Board the Wherry 'Zoe', and its Tender, the Tub, 'Lotus'.* The 110 page book, with twenty-two fine illustrations by Wilfrid Ball plus several folding maps showing the route taken, tells of the trials and tribulations of the two boats with Rye and his friends on the *Lotus* accompanying the *Zoe*, presumably hired at short notice from Harry Brittain, on which were an American couple who were correspondents of Rye and here to undertake genealogical research. A second edition excludes the reference on page 91 to the suicide

Summer outing to Norwich and the Broads, July, 1902.

of banker, Col. Harvey of Crown Point, a libel action having been threatened.

Without doubt Walter Rye and Harry Brittain would have been professionally acquainted, but it seems that their mutual love for the Broads frequently brought them together. At about this time there was a legal controversy as to public access to a number of the Broads – the right to fish, and the limitations of the public to row and sail. Rye writes in his autobiography: "The first aggressors had been Blofield of Hoveton, who chained up the two entrances of Hoveton, and Blake Humphrey, who got a conviction for a man fishing on Wroxham." A Norfolk Broads Protection Society was formed to fight the public case, with Walter Rye as its hon. Solicitor. In defence, Brittain and Rye were as one: in his preface to the second edition of ***Notes on the Broads and Rivers of Norfolk & Suffolk (1888)*** Brittain wrote: "I must again warn my readers that the 'Land of the Broads' is not altogether a district where unlimited licence may be taken. The very large liberty formerly allowed by the riparian owners has, I regret to say, been so much abused that, to protect their obvious rights, many have closed their waters.... It happens that some alarmists locally are beginning to raise the cry 'that all the Broads will soon be closed'. I hope this absurd statement may not gain ground outside the county, as it is most assuredly an exaggeration, for in many instances the public have inalienable rights of navigation."

1891 saw the case came to court, though not altogether favourably, and in the following year Rye wrote *The Rights of Fishing, Shooting, and Sailing on the Norfolk Broads Considered by Walter Rye*. The 113 page book was published by Jarrold & Sons in light-grey printed boards and was an attempt to give the reader the rights and wrongs of the public's case, and an outline of the proceedings in court.

Further co-operation between Brittain and Rye was evident in the 1902 visit of the Quatuor Coranati Lodge to Norwich. In the transactions *Summer Outing – Norwich 3rd to 6th July, 1902* it tells of how the members were entertained at the Maids Head by Walter Rye who was to act as guide and interpreter during their sojourn. Harry Brittain, with a Mr Algar, prepared a lantern slide show of the next day's tour in Norwich. Subsequent to that a tour of broadland on board the *Queen of the Broads* was undertaken with the accompaniment of both Rye and Brittain. The description of the tour, published in the transactions, was accompanied by illustrations from Wilfrid Ball's sketches of broadland scenes.

Walter Rye contributed to two further publications relating to the Broads: his *A History of Norfolk*, published in 1885, devotes thirty pages to this district, and in 1893, A H Goose published *The Hickling Broad Case: Micklethwait v Vincent* which was compiled by Rye.

P H EMERSON

As can be seen from previous chapters, personalities such as Davies and Suffling appreciated the Broads of Norfolk and Suffolk so much so that they wished to share their knowledge with others by writing. In this they found support from publishers such as Jarrold & Sons who it can be said mined a seam of the hitherto ignorant public (ignorant in so much as in lacking knowledge of this formerly unpublicised haven). Both also wrote extensively on other subjects, including fiction. A larger than life character, Walter Rye's first love was researching and it seems that he wrote so he could publicise his findings, with many of his booklets being printed in small limited editions. His publications ran into hundreds, and the Broads would have played only a small part in his extraordinary life.

P H (Peter Henry) Emerson also wrote many books – several on geneaology of the Emersons, but also Welsh literature, history, nature, biography, billiards, fiction and so on. His legacy, however, was as a result of photography and the publication of his photographically illustrated books, the majority of which were based in East Anglia and, in particular, the Broads. Born in Cuba in 1856 of an American coffee planter father and an English mother, his later schooldays were spent as a border at Cranleigh in Surrey after which he graduated from King's College, London, as a doctor. He did not take the profession further but developed an interest in photography, initially in 1882 as a hobby, but which grew to perhaps an obsession culminating with his theories of photography as an art.

It was whilst Emerson was staying at Southwold, where he 'took several photographs that were destined to revolutionise photography and make my name in photographic circles,' that he had his first introduction to the Broads when, in 1885 with his

Gathering waterlilies from Life and Landscape on the Norfolk Broads by P H Emerson.

brother, he hired the yacht *Emily*. During this sailing trip he also became acquainted with the artist Thomas Frederick Goodall who became a close friend and with whom he collaborated in producing his first photographically illustrated book – *Life and Landscape on the Norfolk Broads* which was published in 1887 (dated as 1886) by Sampson Low, Marston, Searle and Rivington. In oblong format, it was illustrated with forty platinotype photographs and published in two editions: the de-luxe edition, limited to only 25 copies, in a white vellum decorated binding and priced at ten guineas, and the ordinary edition which was limited to 175 copies at a price of six guineas.

From page 128 of The English Emersons, P H Emerson.

The constituent photographs are highly sought after and many copies of the book have been broken so that these could be sold individually for high prices. Intact volumes do come to auction from time to time, with a recent de-luxe copy fetching £35,000 plus buyer's premium at a sale in New York. This title remains by far the most expensive book on the subject of the Broads and exceeds the value of any other by a considerable margin*.

The next few years saw a steady flow of works by Emerson. Generally they were characterised by being published in two editions: a small number of de-luxe copies, usually bound in white vellum with morocco leather spines (which were very prone to wear), and an ordinary cloth edition though in a similar style. The majority would be numbered and signed. *Life and Landscape* was the only publication to contain real photographs with the photogravure being used for illustrating subsequently. This chapter only describes his works that relate to the Norfolk and Suffolk Broads and excludes those covering other parts of East Anglia such as *Pictures from Life in Field and Fen* (1887), *Pictures of East Anglian Life* (1888) and *Wild Life on a Tidal Water* (1890) . Emerson contributed to only one photographically illustrated book from out of the region, that being a new edition of *The Compleat Angler* for which he was commissioned by its editor to take 26 photographs of the River Lea.

Emerson's next work (dated April 1887) was *Idyls of the Norfolk Broads* which was published by the Autotype Company, based at New Oxford Street, London. This was issued within a decorative portfolio as a collection of twelve atmospheric loose photogravures of varying sizes, together with a title page (where Idyls is spelt with a double 'l'), list of contents, four page introductory essay and one page of description to

From page 129 of The English Emersons, Maid of the Mist.

each plate. The de-luxe edition comprised 100 copies (150 were stated), was priced at one pound, eleven shillings and sixpence and issued on India paper. There were a similar number of ordinary copies priced at one guinea. As with **Pictures from Life in Field and Fen**, which was published at about the same time and in the same format, Emerson's portfolios, with their loose plates, almost invited photographic dealers to split the volumes in order to sell the photogravures individually. Hence both titles tend to be scarcer than those issued in conventional book form.

Dating from 1893, and published in book form by David Nutt, **On English Lagoons** was also limited to 100 copies and priced at one pound, five shillings. This, the signed de-luxe edition, was illustrated with fifteen photogravures and an unlimited ordinary edition, unsigned and without the plates, was also published. The full title included the words: 'being an account of the voyage of two amateur wherrymen on the Norfolk and Suffolk Rivers and Broads, with an appendix the log of the wherry *Maid of the Mist* from September 15, 1890, to August 31, 1891' – and the book ran to 298 pages, being chronologically arranged. The ordinary edition was attractively bound in olive-green cloth illustrated with a broadland scene to the top board, whilst the limited edition was of quarto size in plain white buckram with a green and gilt morocco spine. Much to my surprise, an auction box of books offered at a Beccles saleroom, and purchased at the time that my manuscript was being corrected, contained a buff paper-covered version of **On English Lagoons** described on the cover as 'cheap edition 3/- nett'. The title page was dated 1896 with a further qualification as to being 'cheap re-issue'. This edition ran to only 272 pages, plus 4 pages of press reports about Emerson's Birds, Beasts, and Fishes, the log of the *Maid of the Mist* being omitted. Printed to the reverse of the half-title was: 'Copies of the Original Edition of this work are still on sale at 7s 6d, comprising, in addition to the matter contained in the present issue, the Log of the *Maid of the Mist*, from Sept. 15, 1890, to Aug. 31, 1891, with a full record of meteorological and natural history observations. Handsomely bound in cloth cover, printed in colours, uncut. Also a few copies of the large paper issue, printed on small 4to, on hand-made paper, and illustrated with fifteen additional full-page photo-etchings. Handsomely bound in half morocco and buckram, £1 10s Net.'

The coloured illustration to the cover of the original ordinary edition was repeated on the cheap edition, but in black only. This 'cheap' edition appears not to have been previously recorded and I had not previously seen a copy.

Emerson's final photographically illustrated Broads' book was published in 1895, also by David Nutt, and entitled **Marsh Leaves**. It was issued in three editions: a de-luxe edition, limited to100 copies, with sixteen photogravures on Japanese vellum, bound in decorated white cloth with a brown morocco and gilt spine and priced at one guinea; an ordinary edition of 200, retailing at ten shillings and sixpence, with the photogravures on ordinary paper and bound in blue decorated cloth, both editions having 165 pages; and an unlimited 198 page edition of much slighter stature which was published in 1898 without illustrations and in decorated cloth boards.

One other book appeared later which was illustrated with just one photogravure, that being a de-luxe edition of **English Idyls** which comprised a series of essays, some of which were based on the Broads. The original edition without illustrations was published in 1889 by Sampson Low, Marston, Searle, & Rivington Limited in a edition supposedly of only 25 though a reprint was undertaken in the same year. This book was subsequently reprinted in 1924 in a flimsy yellow binding in a numbered edition of 1025, of which 25 de-luxe copies were published in half morocco with gilt decoration to the spine and a photogravure to the frontis which had first appeared as one of the illustrations to *Marsh Leaves*. My copy is a presentation copy with a seven line message from Emerson to a Captain Holt. The late Ernest Webster, a chartered surveyor who had a fine collection of broads' books and whose early working life was that as a clerk to a Great Yarmouth marsh lettings company, could remember dealing professionally with the Holt family. Emerson, through his publisher, intended this to be the first of a 22 volume 'Uniform' edition of his works in this format (both de-luxe and ordinary), however, this endeavour was not proceeded with.

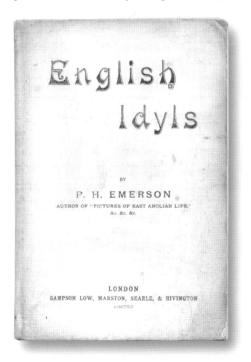

'English Idyls' by P H Emerson, 1889, 1st Edition.

Emerson also wrote a number of other inexpensive books which included broadland content. 1891 saw **East Coast Yarns** with **A Son of the Fens** published the following year, and in 1895, the substantial near 400 page **Birds Beasts and Fishes of the Norfolk Broadland** was published. A second edition (issue) quickly followed and it seems that it was not only in the photographic world that Emerson was controversial and dogmatic.

In a prefatory note he states: "As the author's statement that many of the illustrations were taken from life has been implicitly or explicitly denied by some of his reviewers, it is here emphatically reaffirmed. The author's terminology and classification are not those of official 'natural histories', and some reviewers have assumed that when he differs from the 'authorities' he must be in the wrong. He thinks it well to state that he maintains the accuracy of every fact recorded in the following pages. He has set down nothing save on the warrant of his own observations extending over many years, or on the authority of fowlers, rat catchers, fishermen, gamekeepers, and the like, whose work brings them into daily contact with the birds, beasts, and fishes of the Norfolk Broadland."

1898 saw Emerson's major genealogical work again published by David Nutt. This was **The English Emersons** which also included much broadland content and ran to 168 quarto sized pages with a 135 page appendix. Again this came out in a de-luxe edition of fifty bound in brown morocco backed vellum; there was also a cheaper cloth covered edition. The later years of his writing career saw Emerson concentrate largely on genealogical matters, however, in 1925 he penned a volume of detective stories entitled **The Blood Eagle and Other Tales**. This proved to be his final book, he died in 1936, and whilst it could not be said that he was the most commercially successful writer on the district, he was certainly instrumental in producing the finest books.

* All Emerson's other photographically illustrated works are valuable and worth at least four figures in anything like reasonable condition. A copy of Field and Fen recently fetched over £10,000 and the de luxe copies of his other works generally sell for at least half this amount. Wild Life on a Tidal Water appears to be the most commonly seen and sells for anything between two and four thousand pounds.

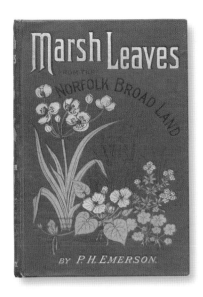

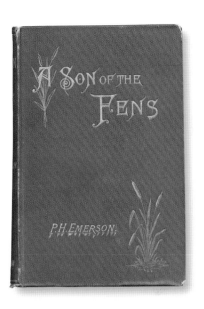

*Marsh Leaves from the Norfolk
Broadland.
Cheap non-illustrated edition.*

A Son of the Fens.

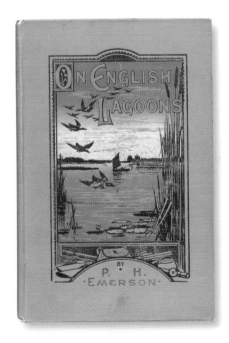

*Birds, Beasts & Fishes of the
Norfolk Broadland.*

*On English Lagoons.
Ordinary edition.*

*Scenes of the Broads from East Anglian Guides, edited by Percy Lindley
for the Great Eastern Railway.*

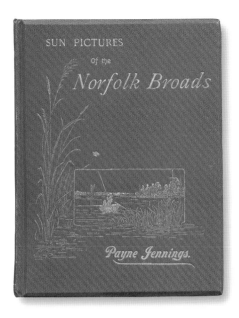

Sun Pictures of the Norfolk Broads.
1st edition.

Sun Pictures of the Norfolk Broads.
3rd edition.

Frontispiece and title page of the 3rd edition
of Sun Pictures of Norfolk.

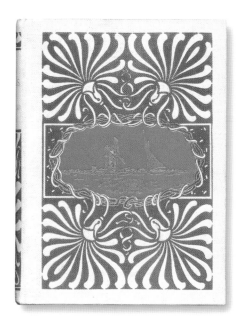

*On the Broads
by Anna Bowman Dodd.*

En Wherry.

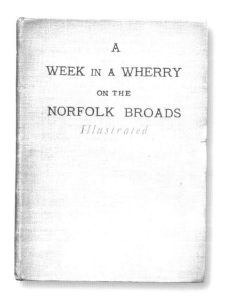

*A Week in a Wherry on the
Norfolk Broads.*

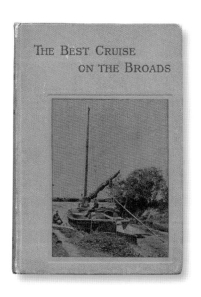

The Best Cruise on the Broads.

PHOTOGRAPHY AND THE THE RAILWAY CONNECTION

A future chapter will detail how the independent railway companies took advantage of the increasing popularity of the Broads in order to promote ticket sales and increase the profitability of their operations. Having already in previous chapters outlined the work of Davies and Emerson and their relationship to the Broads, a third photographer, John Payne Jennings, should now be included and was at work here in the 1880s, probably at the behest of the Great Eastern Railway. Payne Jennings was rather a mystery man, and it seems that he never committed pen to paper, nor had other than a commercial connection with this region. His family, it is said, came from Market Harborough in Leicestershire. What brought him to the Broads was probably as a result of a commercial decision by the GER to expand into the growing holiday resorts of East Anglia, including Broadland. How he came to obtain such a lucrative commission to take photographs for the company is not known, but he seems to have taken full advantage of it as, by the turn of the century, he had become quite affluent and resided at Gayton House, a large mansion in Surrey, which was surrounded by extensive grounds. Initially Payne Jennings' work was seen in the railway carriages themselves, as GER was the first company to enhance their rolling stock with scenic photographic panels. From about 1884 these panels consisted of seven small black and white mounted photographs with the locations written in ink beneath. Later the more traditional oblong view, still photographic, was used until these were later supplanted by coloured prints from works by specially commissioned artists*. Jarrold and Sons initially published some of these early photographs in view books entitled ***Photographs of Norfolk Broads and Rivers***, but not long after, in 1891, ***Sun Pictures of the Norfolk Broads. One Hundred Photographs from Nature of the Rivers and Broads of Norfolk and Suffolk by Payne Jennings*** appeared being 'Printed at the Permanent Photo Printing Works, Ashtead, Surrey' (Payne Jennings' own company). No publisher was named but, apart from a mention of his 'Photo Art Publications', the only advert was a full page for the Great Eastern Railway which included a fares table from London to Norwich, Wroxham, Yarmouth and Lowestoft. It seems unlikely at this stage of his career that Payne Jennings himself could have afforded the cost of publishing these auto gravures, bound in their high quality cloth and gilt binding. The first edition of *Sun Pictures*, was published without text but this was remedied when a second enlarged edition came out the following year, this time with the publisher stated as Jarrold & Sons but still with the GER full page advert. The connection with Jarrolds was further enhanced with one of their authors, Ernest Suffling, being responsible for the text, both

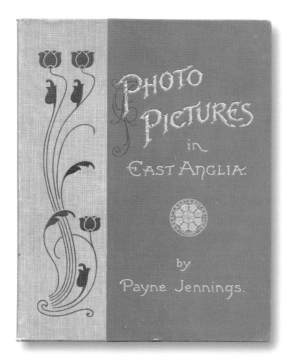

*Photo Pictures in
East Anglia, by
Payne Jennings.*

as an introduction and accompanying each photograph. A cheaper third edition, with the photographs in half tone, was published by Payne Jennings himself in 1897. This still contained the GER advert but now as well had their crest embossed in gilt to the top board. A near identical but cheaper card bound edition was published simultaneously.

At around this time, in a similar style and binding, Payne Jennings also published ***Photo Pictures in East Anglia***. This was also GER crested, but with the letterpress now by Annie Berlyn who also happened also to be a Jarrold's published author (with *Sunrise Land*, and *Vera in Poppyland*). Payne Jennings also photographed and published for other railway companies: ***Summer Holidays in North East England*** for the North Eastern Railway Company, and in 1911 ***Scenic Beauties in Surrey and Sussex*** for the London, Brighton and South Coast Railway. His photographs also illustrated collective works of famous poets such as Wordsworth and reproductions of his photographs were also much used to illustrate several general and East Anglian topographical works.

* A fine collection of Payne Jennings' carriage photographs can be seen at the Heritage Centre (Local Studies Library) situated on the top floor of the Forum in Norwich.

SAILING HOLIDAYS IN THE 1890s

Tourism by now had been underway in this region for over a decade, with many books published and countless articles appearing in journals such as *The Field* and *Chambers*. Still, however, the urge to relate adventures and misfortunes in print had not been dulled. The holiday maker and boat hirer (plus the very necessary crew or a 'man') was still usually male, from the professional classes and, perhaps considering the printing cost of recording his soujorn for posterity, responsible for an early example of vanity publishing.

The opening year of the decade saw the Leadenhall Press publish ***A Week in a Wherry on the Norfolk Broads by 'Blue Peter', Illustrated by the Purser***. Chapter One opens: 'When we announced to our friends, as a settled plan, that we meant to spend a week in a wherry on the Norfolk Broads, we encountered a storm of ridicule and discouragement. "The latest Cockney tourist's trip," said one. "You will sail at the rate of a mile an hour on muddy ponds and ditches," said another.'

The party was composed of 'four keen whist players' and consisted of 'the Purser and Mrs Purser, the Commodore and Mrs. Commodore'. Their week's trip commenced from Wroxham and the wherry they had hired was the *Kate*.

Horning Ferry from Summer Holidays by Percy Lindley.

The following year, 1891, saw the printing of a quarto-sized paper covered 20 page booklet entitled *The Merry Mariners. An account of the 1891 Summer Outing of the Loddon Young Men's Mutual Improvement Society. By One of Them*. The booklet is subtitled 'Who went for a Sail in a Wherry, which they found Wherry Unsailable'. The text by TWE (Thomas William Ellis) is in verse and interspersed with numerous fairly amateurish drawings of the Mariners and what they observed. The wherry was the *Lady Violet*, and the outing started at Loddon and followed the Chet until it joined the Yare, and then to Buckenham and presumably back.

1892 saw the publication of the only early Broads' book to be written in a foreign language: *EN WHERRY. Trois Semaines dans Les Broads du Norfolk*. Published in Paris, the 171 page lavishly bound volume was illustrated by five heliogravures (printed in different colours) plus a folding map of the Broads. The author was a Count D'Epremesiul from the Chateau de Thisbermount near Dieppe, and he relates a three week excursion through the Norfolk Broads. Jarrold & Sons hoped, in 1893, to publish a limited edition in English in association with James Hooper, however, this was abandoned largely due to the cost.

1895 saw yet another book describing a boating holiday, which again started from Wroxham. *A Week on the Bure, Ant & Thurne* was privately printed in a limited edition by Charles Coleman Laing. Laing had joined three other members of his family, plus skipper Gibb, on the yacht *May Fly* for a relaxing sketching holiday undertaken the previous August. My copy is numbered 41 and a presentation copy from Laing, though there is no indication of the limitation to the edition. This is, however, one of the scarcest and in a way, one of the most bizarre, books written about a trip on the Broads.The narrative is in the first person singular and relates all sorts of trivia as far as the holiday is concerned. In this it is not unusual; what is, is that Laing is called back to London for a meeting at the Stock Exchange and tells in its gory detail of what he found when he returned to his residence at Queen's Gate. After his meeting, Laing returns to his holiday, catching the Potter Heigham train from Liverpool Street. Unfortunately (for him) it is August and space in First Class is full and he relates: "It was a third-class compartment and full with a grandmother, a brace of parents, their eldest daughter, her young man, and a posse of children down to the baby. They had already begun tea and were giving a briny flavour to the heated atmosphere by shelling shrimps and extracting winkles. They were all in boisterous spirits and disagreeably warm, but an annual outing does not come every day. They kindly made as much room for me as they could in a corner. And offered me refreshment but I declined their nutriment."

The story of the train journey then takes a twist – but before he finishes the tale Laing wakes up to the sound of: "Wake up Uncle, Joseph has caught a fish and kicked over the claret cup!" It was all a dream, but does rather emphasise the class that were still hiring boats for their holidays in the 1890s.

Charles Henry Cook, who wrote under the name of John Bickerdyke, was a prolific writer of books about fishing and also, to a lesser extent, of novels and legends. The Broads did not escape his notice with the publisher Bliss, Sands and Foster bringing out his **The Best Cruise on the Broads** in 1895. Subtitled 'with useful hints on Hiring, Provisioning, and Manning the Yacht; Clothing; Angling; Photography; etc, etc.' this book could be perhaps more described as a guidebook rather than the telling of the story of the trip that Cook actually undertook.

In the preface he says: "Of course, an infinity of books have been written about the Broads: that goes without saying. I bought a whole library, and, moreover, studied them diligently, before making my first visit to these curious waterways. When on the Broads, I found the excellent guides of Mr Christopher Davies, and other authors, of the greatest service. But I had considerable difficulty in determining which was the best cruise to take, for I had no wish to waste my time sailing along narrow and uninteresting rivers."

Walter Rye in his Songs, Stories, and Sayings rather took Cook to task for penning a book with such an arrogant title, particularly since it was 'the result of something under a week's experience'.

One further book in this decade which related a trip on the Broads was published in 1896 by Macmillan and Co Ltd. **On the Broads** was written by Anna Bowman Dodd and had in fact seen the light of day the previous year in volume fifty of the *Century Magazine*. In book form it ran to 331 pages and was illustrated by Joseph Pennell, one of the illustrators to the successful Highways and Byways series. It was lavishly and substantially bound in an art nouveau decorated style which framed a gilt and powder-blue vignette of a wherry and windmill. The story starts at Wroxham with the hiring of the yacht *Vacuna*, its crewing and provisioning (seemingly to the advantage of every tradesman in the village), and continues with the usual antics of the gentlemen hirers and their local 'river and boat-wise' crew. From Wroxham the cruise takes in Hickling and Horsey, Yarmouth and then the Yare to Norwich, with Cantley Regatta on the way. In many respects the book is written in the style of a novel and perhaps is not as well regarded as some. Walter Rye in his **Songs, Stories, and Sayings** sarcastically commented that 'an American lady has perpetrated a book on the subject, giving us the benefit of her three or four day's experience'. Rye also adds a further comment about the number of people tempted to write about the Broads; however, twenty years were to pass before the next book in the genre saw publication and then a further thirty years before Reginald James Hewitt privately printed his **Wild Rose**.

JOHN KNOWLITTLE

John Knowlittle was the pen-name for Arthur Henry Patterson who was born in the humble surroundings of a Great Yarmouth row in 1857 and, whilst never losing the privilege of his 'common' upbringing, became a prolific author, accepted by the natural history-loving gentry of the county, a valued friend to the Duchess of Bedford and, in the year of his death in 1935, elected as an Associate of the Linnaean Society, a position open to only twenty five.

Patterson, like several of his contemporaries, wrote on many subjects – monkeys, zoos, fish, birdlife, shadow entertainments, Methodism, his life as a school attendance officer, the Broads and in particular the natural history of his beloved Breydon. He was also a cartoonist and, apart from his well known 'lightning' sketches of birds and the like, he contributed hundreds of cartoons for publication in the *Yarmouth Mercury*. This chapter is not intended to be about his writings in general, nor about the several natural history works he penned on Yarmouth and Breydon waters, but is limited to the books he wrote specifically about the Broads.

In his fifty years as a writer, Patterson saw the printing of his manuscripts by many publishing houses, from the small local stationer to such as Methuen who embraced all the countries of the British Empire. Nothing would seem more natural than for Jarrold and Sons to take him

Arthur Henry Patterson

Bookplate designed and drawn by A H Patterson.

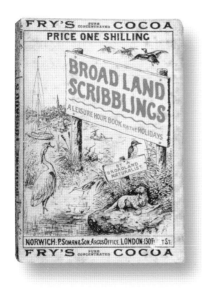

Broadland Scribblings
by A H Patterson.

under their wing and they so did with his first proper book which was entitled **Seaside Scribblings for Visitors** and which they published in 1887. However, with the exception of **Charles H Harrison Broadland Artist** it was to be 35 years before he returned to Jarrolds with **The Cruise of the Walrus**, and in 1892 he turned to P Soman and Son at the 'Argus' office in Norwich to publish his first book based on the Broads. **Broadland Scribblings, a Leisure Hour book for the Holidays by a Broadland Naturalist** was very much in the same style and format as its seaside predecessor and was published in card boards, with a typical Patterson drawing to the cover, at the price of 1/-. Its 198 pages of text was supplemented by many local adverts. Several of Patterson's books are extremely scarce and fetch very high prices when they come onto the market. *Broadland Scribblings* is certainly one of these and even when it does appear it is seldom in other than poor condition. It seems likely that the very fact that he was published by so many obscure firms, who must have lacked the distribution systems that were open to companies such as Jarrold and Methuen, that has led to the rarity of so many of his works.

Three years later in October 1895, Thomas Mitchell of Aldersgate Street, East London, published Patterson's month to month sketches about the people and bird-life of broadland, commencing of course in January and proceeding to the year end. These sketches it seems had appeared in the **Primitive Methodist Magazine** during the preceding year, but put together in bookform they made a very acceptable 143 page quarto sized volume. Entitled **Man and Nature on the Broads** this very attractive book was bound in cloth and gilt with decoration in black and a circular silver insert of a boating scene to the top board. As with several nineteenth century broadland volumes, this was issued in varying coloured boards.

Arthur Patterson's preface summed up the now popularity of the district against that of the early 1880s: "Ten years ago a book on Broadland would have needed a lengthy introduction – the likeness of its spreading lagoons, their whereabouts, attractions, and delights would have required treatment in detail to have become intelligible to many who live outside the county that boasts their possession. Now everybody knows them, many by a personal inspection, most by repute. In summer crowds of yachting folk, and excursionists by rail, steamer, and road, visit these reed – surrounded, coot-haunted waters. But to know them thoroughly is to visit them at every season of the year – a privilege beyond the means or possibilities of all save the favoured few who live upon the spot."

The first decade of the twentieth century saw Patterson at his most prolific with several volumes published by Methuen on the subject of the natural history in the region of his beloved Breydon Water, as well as a book about Primitive Methodism in Great Yarmouth. All these volumes, as well as the half a dozen he wrote after the Great War, were sold in quite large numbers and hence are now relatively inexpensive. The same cannot be said for the slim 60 page volume that he wrote together with A H Smith and which was limited to 175 numbered copies. ***Charles H Harrison, Broadland Artist*** was issued by Jarrold & Sons in 1903 as a memoir to the life of this now appreciated and collected artist who died at the age of sixty in November of the previous year. The book included several black and white reproductions of his paintings and related the difficulties of surviving as an artist whose work only attained real popularity after his death. Like Patterson, Charles Harmony Harrison was born in one of Yarmouth's notorious rows, and he never attained success as a scholar other than artistically. An exhibition, a tribute to his work, had been arranged by a committee of thirty-four members, Arthur Patterson included, to honour the artist who regretfully died one month before it was opened. A catalogue ***The 'Harrison Exhibition', held at The Tolhouse Museum, December, 1902*** was issued and included a potted biography, photograph of the artist as well as a number of lithographs taken from his broadland paintings. 309 works were lent by various contributors, all of which are listed.

   Other than articles, Arthur Patterson did not return to writing full length books about the Broads until after the war, and it is my intention to further describe these when a companion volume is published in due course.

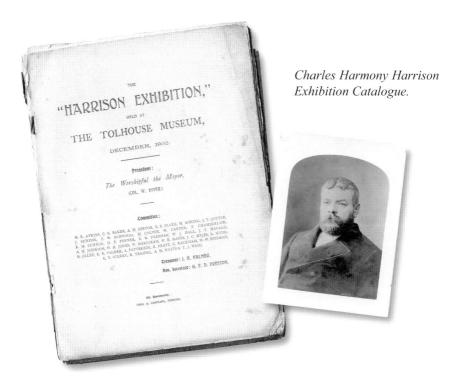

Charles Harmony Harrison Exhibition Catalogue.

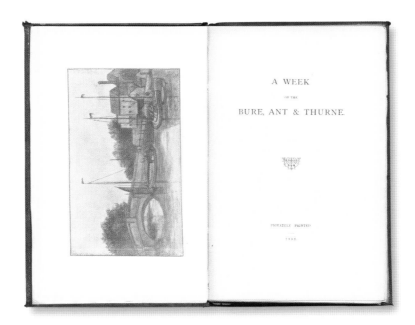

Frontispiece and title page of A Week on the Bure, Ant & Thurne.

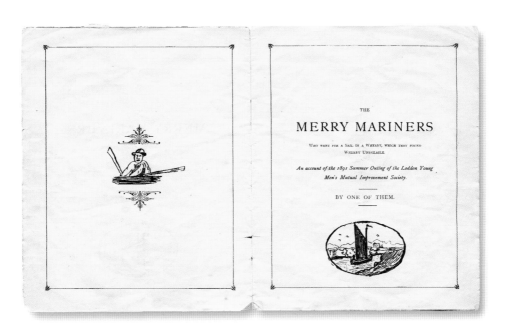

Frontispiece and title page of The Merry Mariners.

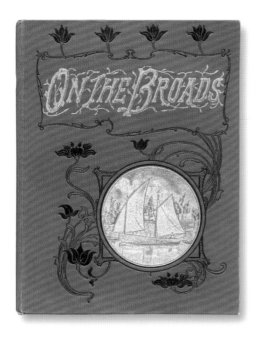

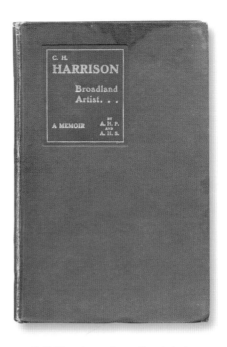

On the Broads by Arthur Patterson.   *G H Harrison, Broadland Artist.*

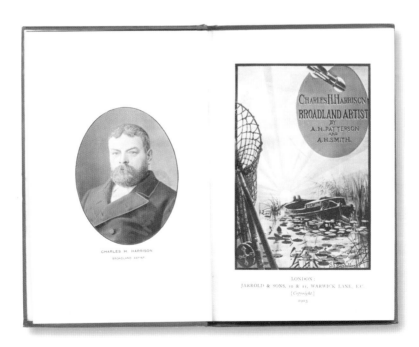

Frontispiece and title page of Broadland Artist.

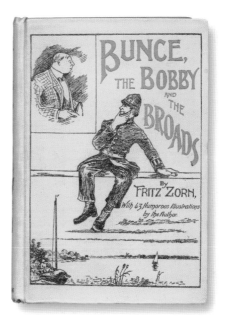

High Jinks, a Tale of the Norfolk
Broads.

Bunce the Bobby and the Broads.

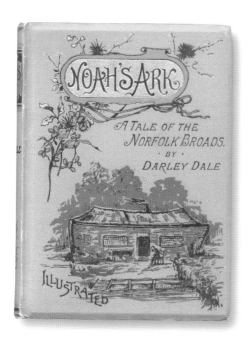

Noah's Ark, a Tale of the Norfolk Broads
by Darley Dale.

The Innocents on the Broads
by Ernest R Suffling.

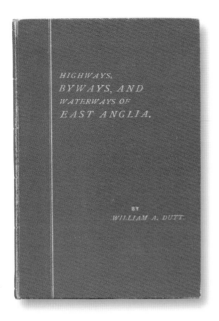

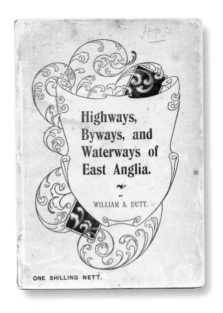

Highways, Byways, and Waterways of East Anglia.

Highways, Byways, and Waterways of East Anglia. Paperback edition.

Frontispiece and title page of The Norfolk Broads.

BROADLAND NOVELS

Possibly the best that can be said of novels written about a century or so ago is that they were generally attractively produced in colourful decorated bindings and look well on a bookcase. In the reading they have not always passed the test of time, with those based on the Broads being no exception. Hence rather than detailing plots and characters, this chapter is more of a listing; however, the lack of readability has not prevented copies becoming very collectable and, with some titles, very scarce.

The broadland novels by Wilkie Collins and George Christopher Davies, both of which are still read today, have been outlined in earlier chapters. It took about fourteen years, during which time the region steadily became more identified by the general public, before a further novel followed the path taken by the *Swan and her Crew*. Both were published by Frederick Warne and Co but *Noah's Ark, a Tale of the Norfolk Broads* by Darley Dale certainly did not reach the heights of its predeccessor, being issued in only one 280 page edition which came out in about 1890.

The following year saw the printing of Ernest Tunbridge's *High Jinks: a Yarn of the Norfolk Broads*. This was produced by the East Norfolk Printing Company situated in Regents Street, Great Yarmouth, and, with no publisher indicated, may have been a private venture by the author. Whatever, it is very scarce and is also very readable being in the style of the 'holiday cruise on the Broads' books featured in the previous chapter.

In 1896, Gordon Stables ('the Gentleman Gipsy') a prolific author of books for 'young readers', wrote *The Cruise of the Rover Caravan* which was published by James Nisbet & Co, Limited. This was the story of the adventures and travels of a horse-drawn gipsy caravan and its occupants. The journey took in many regions including the Broads which is covered in two chapters of the book: "They drove on next day to Rollesby Broad, bivouacking long before noon at another cosy inn, in order to spend a long summer's day or two on Rollesby and Ormsby Broads." Stables also wrote *Leaves from the Log of a Gentleman Gypsy* which was much in the same format.

Jarrold and Sons entered this market in 1900 with **Bunce, the Bobby and the Broads. A Holiday Yarn** by Fritz Zorn, who also provided the '43 Humerous Illustrations' which illustrate the text. It was written in an amusing style and runs to 262 pages. Press reviews were positive with the *Daily Telegraph* reporting: 'A story written with the exclusive object of making its readers laugh...', and the *Norfolk Chronicle:* 'There is not a dull page to be found in it, and to those who are at all acquainted with the Norfolk Broads the scenes described should awaken pleasant memories of many a familiar spot.'

Sales were brisk and very quickly dictated a second and third edition.

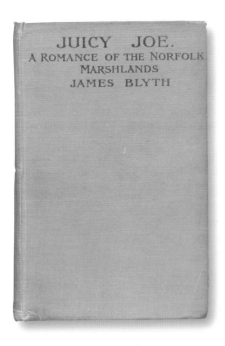

Juicy Joe, a Romance of the Norfolk Marshlands.

By 1902 a cheap edition was published on poor quality paper bound either in a plain cloth or with black-ruled and decorated card boards. Both versions were marked '18th Thousand'. Jarrolds published a complete series of these cheaper style reprints among which was 'Seaside Scribblings' by Arthur H. Patterson.

A previous chapter outlined the works of Ernest Suffling and his very popular books about the Broads. He was also a novelist and wrote at least seven boys adventure books, though only one was based in his favourite region. **The Innocents on the Broads** came out in 1901, again being published by Jarrold & Sons. In the introduction Suffling writes: "The experience of nearly forty years on the land and on the water of the district, cannot have failed to give the writer many happy hours, and to have brought before him many amusing incidents worthy of record. He therefore begs to lay these before his indulgent readers in the hope of giving them a little innocent amusement, as a salt wherewith to flavour the dull round of everyday, workaday, grind away life."

The original edition was published in decorated boards, but other, possibly later, editions were generally to be found in plainer cloth bindings.

James Blyth also penned novels based on this district and **Juicy Joe, a Romance of the Norfolk Marshlands**, published in 1903 by Grant Richards, is one of the scarcest and most sought after. It was published in plain red cloth with the title in gilt and black. It is quite likely that copies when new would have had some form of dust jacket, however, it is rarely seen even without. James (Jas) Blyth in his preface puts the area, and in particular the people who lived there, in a most negative light: 'Everyone for himself and the devil take the hindmost', 'the more regular the church or chapel goer the greater the hypocrite' and 'Often enough have I stayed in country houses (ie with the gentlefolk in residence at the hall) and thought how pleasant, honest, and good the peasants were. How pure the women looked! How sweet and fresh the girls! It was not till I had lived amongst them as one of themselves that I got to know how rotten is the real state of their life when once the hypocrisy is lifted.' Blyth goes on to say that 'although this story belongs to the realms of pure fiction, I have drawn my characters from life as they came to me. I have not picked and chosen with any wish to depict the worst'. It is not for me to say whether Blyth with Juicy Joe gave a true representation of the ordinary people who then inhabited the marshlands of Norfolk, but the 290 page volume, in spoken dialect, does make an entertaining read.

WILLIAM DUTT

William Dutt was a very prolific writer of articles for magazines and journals, but in particular, he wrote several topographies and guidebooks about Norfolk and, to an extent, Suffolk. His published works generally seem to have seen the light of day during the last year or two of the nineteenth century and the first decade of the twentieth. Among his most popular titles were the East Anglian edition of the 'Highways and Byways' series, both the Norfolk and Suffolk 'Little Guides' and the Cambridge and Dent's guides to Norfolk. These, as well as *Wild Life in East Anglia*, all contained chapters which touched on or related to the Broads but are not specific enough to be described here in detail. Dutt also wrote *The King's Homeland* and *The Norfolk and Suffolk Coast*, among others.

His first two titles with broadland content were largely compilations of sketches that he had written for the *Globe* and the *Pall Mall Gazette*, and were reproduced with the permission of their respective editors. Both, **By Sea Marge, Marsh and Mere** (1898) and **Highways, Byways, and Waterways of East Anglia** (1899) contained much broadland material including 'The East Anglian Marshes', 'River Life among the Marshes' and 'Marshland Marginalia', and in the second title 'Among the Marshfolk' and 'Where the Reeds Whisper'. Though both volumes were published in both

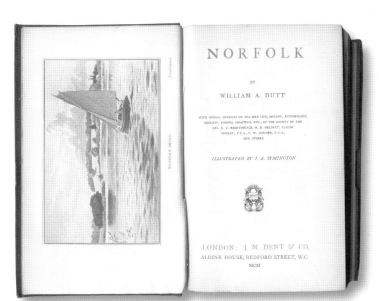

Dent's Guide to Norfolk by William Dutt. Published 1900.

paperback and hardback editions, they are not often seen today in either version, so presumably were printed in relatively small numbers.

Dutt's works were handled by several different publishers, and one of these was Methuen & Co who had undertaken the Little Guide series, with the Norfolk edition having come out in 1902. Methuen's collaboration with William Dutt continued in the following year with what was to become possibly the most successful Norfolk Broads' title ever to see the light of day: *The Norfolk Broads* was written by Dutt himself but also with the assistance of a number of collaborators such as Nicholas Everitt, A J Rudd, James Hooper and Arthur Patterson. The 378 page first edition came out in 1903 in both octavo and larger paper versions and included 48 coloured and 29 uncoloured illustrations from the paintings by the wildlife artist Frank Southgate*. The book was divided into two parts with the first covering the topography of the district, with the remainder covering natural history. Sales dictated a second edition by 1905 with appendices expanding the number of pages to 406. A third edition came out in May 1923 and, by 1930, a fourth revised edition was published. This last edition still had the same number of pages but now was illustrated with 46 colour and 23 uncoloured Southgate plates, as well as 9 other illustrations and 5 maps. A facsimile edition was also published in 2002. All the original editions of *The Norfolk Broads* were in blue cloth with the title and author in gilt to the spine or to the top board, and this is how they are commonly seen. However, what is not generally known is that all editions did originally have dust wrappers which were often discarded by the purchasers, as was the way then. With the early editions this was in the form of a plain brown thick paper wrapper with the title and decoration in red to the spine. The fourth edition (priced at 21/-) had a rather splendid white wrapper, red ruled and with the title etc in blue plus a Southgate colour illustration of a broadland riverside mill to the top cover. I have yet to see a wrapper for the third edition, but this may well have been similar.

There was one other version of this title, that being *A Guide to the Norfolk Broads being Part 1 of the Norfolk Broads*. The blurb to the lower half of the dust wrapper (which again is white with a Southgate colour illustration) states: 'This book – the first half of Mr Dutt's complete work on the Broads – describes those delectable meres in general, with particular passages about the four seasons, the local types, and the wild life'. It was published in 1923 and also has a chapter (Wild Life on Breydon) written by Arthur Patterson. The book runs to 218 pages and includes eight coloured and four uncoloured Southgate plates.

* Methuen also published a number of books by Arthur Patterson in the early years of the twentieth century, and which were written on the theme of natural history in Eastern Norfolk. Some of these were also illustrated by Frank Southgate, as was Dutts 'Wild Life in East Anglia' (1906). Southgate's and Methuen's collaboration was continued further afield with the publication of 'The Romance of Northumberland' in 1908. For this work Frank Southgate provided sixteen splendid colour illustrations.

HANDBOOKS
AND GUIDEBOOKS

S ome very popular guides and handbooks have already been outlined in preceding chapters when penned by the authors so featured. In this chapter are some of the other volumes which were published with the aim of assisting visitors and those intending to sail on these waters. The earliest of these was published well before the turn of the century, with one, first published in 1909, being continually in print until the 1970s .

Circa 1894 saw Iliffe & Son publish H H Warner's *Holiday Tramps through Picturesque England & Wales*. This typical little guidebook ran to some 300-plus pages and covered most of the tourist regions of the country with two of its nine chapters covering those in East Anglia. Chapter eight was almost entirely devoted to the Broads and written in narrative, being a holiday that the author and his family actually undertook (or claimed to).

"The thing to do is to take a wherry. I had splendid fun on the Broads with three other fellows in my bachelor days. On referring to the illustrated pamphlet entitled *Summer Holidays in the Land of the Broads* published by the G E R Company, we found that we could obtain a capital boat for about £5 per week. A long list of boats and of whom they may be hired is given, and I soon became enthusiastic."

There follows a day by day description of the holiday they undertook, with their friends the Franklins, on board the fictitious wherry *Waterwitch* hired at Oulton Broad. The author's introduction to the guide does make the point that it is composed in the narrative form 'because it is largely based on his own personal experiences, and events have been related much as they really occurred'.

In 1900 Jarrold & Sons published *Norfolk Waterways. A Guide to the Navigable Waterways of the Norfolk Broad District, Compiled after a Personal Survey of the Whole* by Henry Rodolph De Salis. De Salis wrote a number of books about inland waterways and their navigation, and in this slim 65 page volume he stated: "This work is not intended to take the place of any of the excellent descriptive Guide Books to the Norfolk Broad District, but to place before the navigator in a handy and concise form, complete information for his travels in this region, much of which has not before been published."

Originally priced at 1/- and published in printed card boards, copies of this book are scarce and do not often come onto the second-hand market.

From time to time during the twentieth century some boat hire companies issued their own guides to the Broads, either complimentary for their clients or perhaps for resale. The earliest that I have noted is **Yachting on the Norfolk Broads** which can be dated to 1901 by the railway adverts for both the Great Eastern and the Great Northern Railways contained within. Apparently written by a Dr H S Lunn of Endsleigh Gardens, Euston, in London (who also advertised his world travel business), the company that produced this 26 page illustrated booklet was the Norfolk Broads Yachting Co, Ltd of Queen Street, Norwich (and stated as 'Known hitherto as H Little & Co, Limited'). A subsequent booklet, probably dating from a few years later and now only with 14 pages plus illustrations and with the same title, was also issued by Henry Little & Co, Ltd (marked 'with the compliments of '). This had no railway adverts to date it, nor in fact any adverts for the hire company or for Dr Lunn, but several for shops and cafés. By now, Henry Little had removed from Norwich to Brundall.

Ward Lock & Co had been extensively publishing guidebooks for all parts of the British Isles since the latter part of the nineteenth century. Locally guides were produced with titles such as Norwich, Cromer, Sheringham, Great Yarmouth, Lowestoft and so on, though the information in these editions did very much tend to overlap. Nicknamed 'red guides,' they were produced in their millions in the familiar limp round-cornered red cloth, with the titles etc in black, and were priced at 1/-. They usually contained several folding maps and had many local and national adverts following the text. It was to the base of these advertising pages where it could be ascertained the series date, as the title page was often not marked either with the edition or date of publication. **The Broads and Rivers of Norfolk and Suffolk** in this series was apparently first issued in 1909/10 and continued in revised forms until relatively recently. The section about the Broads initially ran to 64 pages and gave not only topographical information but also details on hiring with plans of the different type of craft available. A further section, also running to 64 pages, covered Yarmouth and district and also touched on other parts of Norfolk (the specific Yarmouth edition was actually entitled **Yarmouth and the Broads**). At the back were about 90 pages of adverts from national advertisers and these presumably also appeared throughout the series nationwide. A few adverts were placed before the main text and some of these were of a more local nature.

Ward Lock, though by far the most successful, did not have it all its own way in the competition for the increasingly growing guidebook market. At least two other series had widespread sales and ran to several editions in the latter part of the nineteenth and early decades of the twentieth centuries. These included the 'Through Guide Series' published by Thomas Nelson and Sons with **The Eastern Counties with a Practical Section on the Rivers and Broads** (first published 1883), and Murray's **Handbook for Essex, Suffolk, Norfolk and Cambridgeshire** (with editions for 1870, 1875 and 1892). Both, as did many other more localised volumes, contained limited sections about the Broads but these tended to get rather lost among the wealth of information about cities, towns, cathedrals, churches, colleges, tours and the like.

One other publisher did undertake a series which included a title specific to broadland. This was the 'Darlington's handbooks', edited by Ralph Darlington who, according to Geo Stephen, published their **The Norfolk Broads** in 1900. Like Ward

Lock, Darlington's list of British guides was extensive and, though much thinner, were in a similar format. My volume runs to only 80 pages plus the adverts which are mainly for hotels, though the coverage is reasonably extensive. Considering that there were several editions, 1909 and 1912 have been noted with mine dated to 1919 (from the building of a new hotel), copies are infrequently seen. As previously stated, many other publishers brought out topographical volumes for the regions and for individual counties such as Norfolk and Suffolk. All would have included either sections or chapters on the Broads, but my intention is to include only books specifically written about or based on the Broads or, as with the following book, which have some features worthy of inclusion.

Untrodden English Ways by Henry C Shelley was a well-produced 341 page volume published in 1910 by Siegle, Hill & Co and printed in Boston, apparently for the American market. The green cloth binding was expensively tooled in gilt with not only the title, author and publisher, but also three magnificent vignettes to the top board showing life as it would have been then in rural England. All three could relate to broadland – a boating scene, a typical broadland mill and a hay cart reminiscent of a Norfolk farm. The author stated in his preface: "He (the Reader) will know more of England than the average Englishman and greatly exceed the knowledge of the most zealous tourist, if he can claim to have trodden many of these ways .... To the author those byways have always possessed a subtler charm than the highways of common knowledge." Chapter XIII is titled 'The Norfolk Broads' and well illustrated both by line drawings and with sepia photographic reproductions.

Included in this chapter is a book very much of the how to do it genre. ***Comfort in Small Craft. A Practical Handbook of Sailing and Cookery*** by S J Housley was published by John Murray in 1911. Despite its somewhat general title, the author has written the book specifically for those who contemplated venturing onto the waters of this region: "So much has been written justly about the delights of a holiday spent in sailing upon the Norfolk rivers and similar waters, that I need not add another voice to the chorus of enthusiasm. But I would draw attention to a point which has not received all the appreciation it deserves, to wit, that sailing in such waters provides the best training for a beginner that could well be devised.... The rivers of Norfolk are a judicious schoolmaster. They give the pupil plenty of exercises, corrected by mild punishment for mistakes due to inexperience."

The 128 pages continue in this vain of education for the beginner. Clearly a need for such a book was well established, for by 1925, Blake's Ltd had purchased the copyright from the author and republished in an identical format under their own imprint at Broadland House, 22 Newgate Street, London, EC1. An expanded revised edition, with the addition of how to run a motor cruiser, was published by them in 1930.

In 1919, just before my 1920 'cut-off' date, Jarrolds brought out a small 42 page (plus illustrations and adverts) paper-covered booklet entitled ***The Norfolk Broads Handbook***. This, like some of the late Christopher Davies variants, was compiled by Lt-Col R F Lush; however, to complicate matters, on the paper cover was printed in large letters ***Jarrold's Compact Guide to the Rivers and Broads*** with the name of

James Hooper beneath. Possibly this was a post first world war composite rushed out to fill a hoped for surge in the market. It is very rarely seen so perhaps was not a success.

One final volume, written in narrative in the style of 'my visit to' rather than in the form of a guidebook, is *A Summer Sojourn on the East Coast* by 'Luberta' (actually William Waters Spelman). Published in 1892 by the stationer J Rochford O'Driscoll, whose shop at Dagmar House was next to the railway station at Lowestoft, this 255 page book was divided into two parts – the first *Ten Days at Lowestoft*, with the second part similarly *Ten days at Yarmouth*. Both parts included chapters relating to visits to the Broads: Oulton Broad, Fritton Decoy, Ormesby Broad, a cruise on the Bure and Yare, and excursions by river, rail and road. It seems that Spelman also compiled a volume about Lowestoft porcelain in 1905, but of more interest is that he also had O'Driscoll publish in 1892 *A List of the Fishes of the Great Yarmouth District* under his pseudonym, and claimed copyright. However, it appears that in fact Arthur Patterson actually wrote the text.

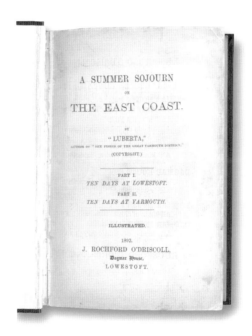

Ten Days at Lowestoft,
Ten Days at Yarmouth,
by Luberta.

Darlington's Handbook: The Norfolk Broads.

Yachting on the Norfolk Broads.

Norfolk Waterways.

Holiday Series No. 1: Holiday Tramps.

Comfort in Small Craft.

HANDBOOKS & GUIDEBOOKS

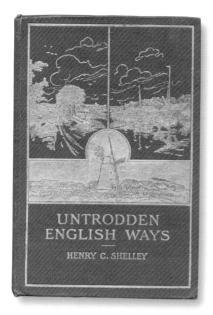

*Untrodden English Ways
by Henry C Shelley.*

TWO MAJOR VOLUMES

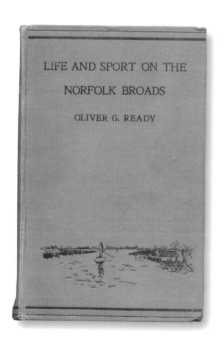

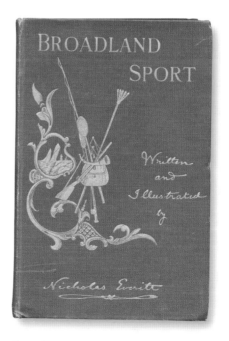

*Life and Sport on the Norfolk
Broads by Oliver G Ready.*

*Broadland Sport by Nicholas Everitt.
Ordinary edition.*

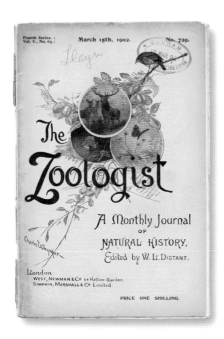

The Zoologist, A Monthly Journal of Natural History.

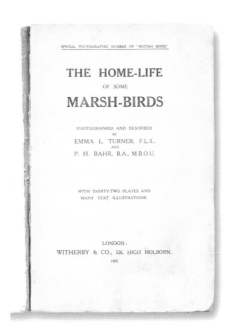

The Home-Life of Some Marsh Birds

Rough Notes on Natural History in Norfolk & the Eastern Counties.

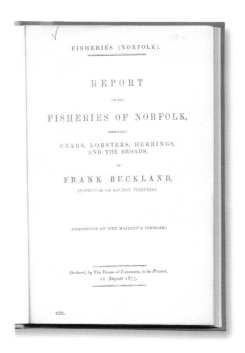

Report of the Fisheries of Norfolk.

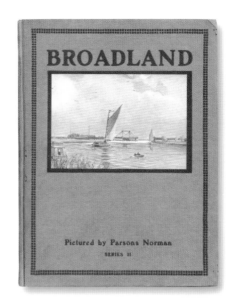

Broadland, Series 1.

Broadland, Series II.

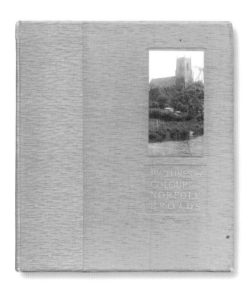

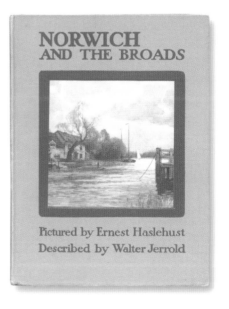

Pictures in Colour of the Norfolk Broads.
Published by Jarrolds.

Norwich and the Broads.

TWO MAJOR VOLUMES

There are several 'highlights' when considering broadland literature: Christopher Davies with his *Handbook* and Ernest Suffling with *Land of the Broads* always readily come to mind. Walter Dutt's long in print *Norfolk Broads*, with its many fine colour plates from the watercolours of Frank Southgate, has certainly stood the test of time. Plates from Peter Emerson's magnificent, and prohibitively expensive, photographic works are frequently reproduced to epitomise broadland scenery. However, as a bookseller specialising in this subject, I was always well aware that when I had copies in stock of the two books described in this chapter they would not only create much interest but soon go out of the door wrapped up in the proverbial brown paper bag.

The first of these, published in 1902 by R A Everett & Co, was **Broadland Sport**, written and illustrated by Nicholas Everitt, whose name is immortalised in the Oulton Broad park donated by him for the public good. The unlimited 'ordinary' edition is a satisfactorily weighty 393 page volume bound in green cloth with superb gilt

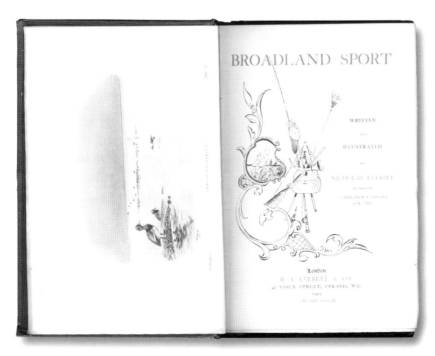

Title page and frontispiece of Broadland Sport.

decoration to the boards. Everitt's preface tells of the intention of giving the reader a trustworthy account and description of the sport obtained on and around the lagoons, waterways and marshlands of Broadland. This volume, he affirms, does not clash with any other volume previously published, being exclusively devoted to the subject of sports and pastimes in this interesting district.

A number of the chapters were based on articles written by the author in such periodicals as *The Field*, *Land and Water*, *The Shooting Times* and *Rod and Gun*. The friends and collaborators listed who assisted Nicholas Everitt in collecting information for the book reads like a Who's Who in the business and professional world, those communities of course then being very much to the fore in the shooting, fishing and sailing worlds of East Anglia. Chapters detail eel bobbing, decoys, wildfowling, punt-gunning, tench tickling, pike fishing, otter hunting and so on, as well as yachts and yachting from the early days to the present.

There were three editions all published in 1902. The ordinary edition, outlined above, was printed in May 1902 but completely sold out before publication necessitating a second impression which came out the following month. A facsimile of this was published as recently as 2002. A footnote to the ordinary edition stated 'An Edition de Luxe is also issued, demy 4to on specially manufactured art paper, with Frontis piece and numerous full-page Plates in Photogravure, limited to 100 copies, each numbered and signed by the Author, price Two Guineas net.' This magnificent 'large-paper' edition was bound in half vellum and all the pages bordered with red-ruling. It also contained eleven superb photogravures, not present in the ordinary edition, which were taken from illustrations by Everitt himself. It also appears that there were a number of unsigned copies of the de luxe edition, in an identical vellum binding, that were sold without the gravure plates and not numbered. It may be assumed perhaps that these were 'out of edition' copies and possibly sold at a lower price, but nevertheless they are still fine volumes.

Nicholas Everitt wrote several other books unrelated to this district, including: *Shots from a Lawyer's Gun* (which ran to several editions), *Ferrets; Their Management in Health and Disease*, *Practical Notes on Grasses and Grass Growing* and so on. One **Told by Twilight** published in 1904 in decorated cloth boards, had illustrations by A J Munnings and consisted of essays and sketches, some of which were based on the Broads.

The second 'highlight' described in this chapter was published in 1910 by T Werner Laurie and entitled **Life and Sport on the Norfolk Broads in the Golden Days** by Oliver G Ready BA.

Oliver Ready's nostalgic 'Author's Note' reads: "I cannot believe that any other boy ever had so happy and so interesting a childhood as myself, with the sea on one side, the dear old Broad on the other, and the kindest of friends at every turn. The remembrance of those golden days midst old-time surroundings, which, alas, have now vanished never to return, has ever been to me a constant source of pleasure and companionship, but especially so during spells of service in the Far East, where in writing these pages, I have turned long nights of loneliness into fair days by the old

Broad, revisiting old haunts and revelling in the companionship of former playmates."

If, by some form of magic, Oliver Ready was to now, one hundred years on, write his note, would he qualify those 'golden days'; would he even recognise the broadland of today as that of his youth?

Chapter headings relate to the usual fishing, sailing and shooting, but also ratting and rabbiting, birds' nests and, unsurprisingly, his boyhood recollections. There are a number of splendid photographic illustrations, several of which were taken by Yallops from Great Yarmouth. The frontis plate, taken by Miss Emma Turner, is of a Coot and a Great Crested Grebe nesting only a foot or two apart. The book also contains two pages of 'Vocabulary', that is a listing of words in Norfolk dialect with their translation.

This desirable book was issued in an olive-green cloth binding with title and an illustration in black to the top board and gilt to the spine. Far more rarely seen is the 'paperback' edition, contemporary with the case bound version, but otherwise identical and bound in printed olive-green thick paper covers.

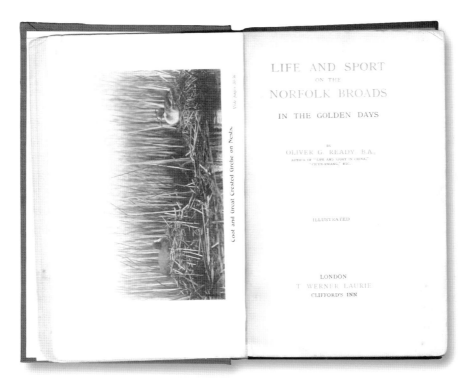

Life and Sport on the Norfolk Broads – photographic illustration
of Coot and Great Crested Grebe on nests by Miss E L Turner.

NATURAL HISTORY

This chapter describes a few publications written by and for the naturalist rather than, as outlined in the previous chapter, those with the accent more on the shooting, hunting and fishing style of country life.

1890 saw Jarrold & Sons publish H M L's (Colonel Hill Mussenden Leathes) *Rough Notes on Natural History in Norfolk & the Eastern Counties*. Colonel Leathes owned the Herringfleet estate and lived at the hall; he had a great interest in the fauna of the district and recorded his observations in this attractive card bound volume with its cover illustrations of birds, fish and sedges bordering a sketch of Wroxham bridge and a sailing wherry. The content is by no means exclusively about this region but, as a yacht owner and regularly sailing on these rivers, he showed his love for the Broads and also devotes several pages to his appreciation of the skills of the wherryman.

1890 also was the date of the publication of the first volume of *The Field Club: a Magazine of General Natural History for Scientific and Unscientific Readers*. Edited by the Rev Theodore Wood and published by Elliot Stock of Paternoster Row in London, this came out in monthly parts but was also issued in four annual volumes until publication ceased in 1893, when it was incorporated with *Nature Notes, the Magazine of the Selborne Society*. Among the many contributors was the Rev M C H Bird who in 1891 saw the inclusion of the first chapter of his *Bird-Life of the Norfolk Broads*. In the introductory remarks he comments of how well known this district is, so needing no further description. He continues in a more negative vein with comparison of today with years gone by: "Suffice it to say that the everyday bird-life of the Broads is by no means either so varied or so plentiful as it was even twenty years ago, when artificial drainage had contracted the haunts of marsh and water birds just as much as at the present time."

His chapters were continued throughout 31 issues with the last accompanying the editorial which announced the closure of the magazine in 1894.

Emerson's *Birds Beasts & Fishes of the Norfolk Broadland* has already been recorded in the chapter outlining this particular author's works, and, within the date limitations that I have set for this bibliography, there is only one other author who specifically wrote on this subject within this district. That person was the redoubtable Miss E (Emma) L Turner FLS, FZS. In her Presidential Address at the 53rd Annual Meeting of the Norfolk and Norwich Naturalists' Society she reported: "It is twenty years since I first explored the Broadland, and seventeen years since my houseboat was brought by land from Sutton Staithe, and launched on Hickling Broad. On March 18th, 1905, the *Water Rail* made her first voyage, carrying as her crew Mr and Mrs Bird and

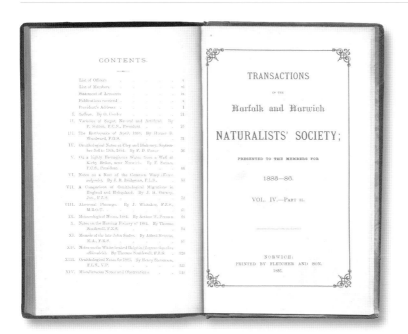

Transactions of the Norfolk and Norwich Naturalists' Society. Published annually,

myself; steered and propelled by Alfred Nudd she came to anchor in the quiet haven, where some of the happiest days of my life have been spent. If you would know people you must live with them, if you want to know birds you must live amongst them...."

Miss Turner's incredibly patient efforts gave rise to the frontis plate in Oliver Ready's *Life and Sport on the Norfolk Broads* but in particular to her first book *The Home-Life of some Marsh-Birds* published in 1907 by Witherby & Co. This 62 page limp bound volume was written with P H Bahr and illustrated by thirty-two fine black and white photographic plates, many having been taken on Hickling Broad.

Whilst specific volumes about the natural history of broadland are few in number, this is more than made up with the presence of two long-running periodicals. The first of these, which is still issued today (and includes the splendid 'Natural History of the Catfield Hall Estate' published in 2009), is the *Transactions of the Norfolk & Norwich Naturalists' Society*. The transactions were first published in 1869 and, throughout the years, have included much of broadland interest as well as specific articles such as 'The Norfolk Broads and Meres Geologically Considered' (J E Taylor, 1871). Membership was drawn extensively from the county professional and land-owning classes, but also from those whose lives were devoted to observation and botanical and zoological research in East Anglia, Arthur Patterson being a prime example. Colonel Leathes, P H Emerson and Miss Emma Turner were members, as were Harry Brittain and Christopher Davies. I understand that a substantial stock of bound early volumes was destroyed by fire, hence these are seldom available for purchase. Individual parts, in their uniform buff printed paper wraps, are more often seen though are scarcer before the 1920s.

The other periodical is *The Zoologist: a Popular Miscellany of Natural History*.

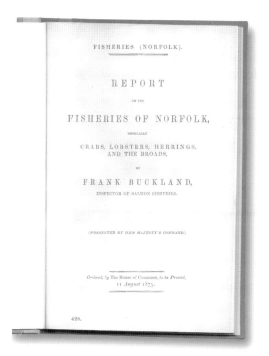

FISHERIES (NORFOLK).

REPORT

ON THE

FISHERIES OF NORFOLK,

ESPECIALLY

CRABS, LOBSTERS, HERRINGS,
AND THE BROADS,

BY

FRANK BUCKLAND,

INSPECTOR OF SALMON FISHERIES.

(PRESENTED BY HER MAJESTY'S COMMAND.)

Ordered, by The House of Commons, to be Printed,
11 August 1875.

428.

Title page of the Report of Fisheries
of Norfolk.

Published by John Van Voorst, the first volume was issued in 1843 and it ran until the first world war. A prolific contributor was Arthur Patterson with others from this district including J H Gurney, Thomas Southwell, T E Gunn, and F Cook from Lowestoft. Articles tended to veer on the Yarmouth/Breydon area rather than pure Broads. Bound volumes, as well as individual issues in the publishers printed wraps, are seen; Arthur Patterson had many of his articles specially bound in printed paper wraps and these are highly collectable, particularly since one or two of his books first saw publication in the columns of the Zoologist.

One other volume worthy of inclusion is ***Notes and Letters on the Natural History of Norfolk more especially on the Birds and Fishes*** which was published by Jarrold & Sons in 1902. This was compiled from the manuscripts of Sir Thomas Browne MD (1605–1682) deposited in the British Museum Library and at the Bodleian, and has notes and an introduction by Thomas Southwell. In addition to Southwell's 26 page introduction, the book further comprises 102 pages with a number of references to the rivers and broads.

Finally, though perhaps the author was not a naturalist in the conventional sense, one particular book, in fact a report, by Frank Buckland should perhaps be mentioned. Buckland's particular study and interest was saltwater fisheries and he was instructed by the Home Office to inquire into the state of the crab, lobster and other sea-coast fisheries on the coast of Norfolk; and ascertain whether they should be placed under regulations to prevent waste, and to preserve them in the future. In his ***Report on the Fisheries of Norfolk*** presented by Her Majesty's Command, to the House of Commons in 1875, he states: "In obedience to your instructions to 'Hold an inquiry into the state of the Crab, Lobster, and other Sea-coast Fisheries on the coast of the County of Norfolk' .... I have held inquiries at the following places: Yarmouth, Cromer, Lynn, Wells, Norwich, Lowestoft, Ludham, and Horning Ferry ....."

Twelve pages of the 84 page report directly relate to *The Broads of Norfolk and Suffolk* in which he gives not only geographical information but also the then proprietors of the individual broads and the dimensions. He proceeds "I have taken evidence from a large number of proprietors and gentlemen directly interested in the Norfolk Broads and their fisheries. It appears that not only the Broads but the navigable rivers connected with them are extensively netted, and the fish sent to inland towns and sold for 1s per stone, or used for manure. Mr Burroughs, of Norwich, states that the interest of the Broads was often divided amongst small proprietors ....."

His report proceeds in this vein, and in doing so gives much valuable information about the district that otherwise may well have been lost. Two other volumes give further information on his visit to Norfolk and the Broads, namely: ***Life of Frank Buckland*** written by his brother-in-law, George Bompas, following Buckland's death in 1880, and ***Notes and Jottings from Animal Life*** arranged by Frank Buckland shortly before his death and published in April 1882. In this volume one chapter is devoted to and entitled *Notes from Yarmouth.*

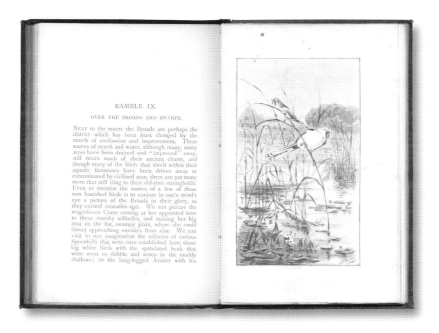

'Over Broads and Swamps' a chapter in The Birds of Our Rambles
by Charles Dixon, 1891. (Not mentioned in the text but a typical example
of a Natural History chapter published in many books at this time).

THE PAINTED SCENE

The Norwich School (of artists) is known the world over for the superb oils and watercolours painted, mainly in the 19th century, by such artists as Crome, Cotman, Stark, Stannard, Vincent and others. The scenery of the rivers and broads of Norfolk and Suffolk were often favourite compositions; as well some artists also produced sets of etchings encompassing broadland scenes. These sets (or collections), either bound in boards or published loose in printed wrappers and with perhaps a list of the contents, are extremely rare and also very expensive if and when they do come onto the market. Whether in book form or otherwise, I feel that they are beyond inclusion in this bibliography. In this chapter thus are books which comprise collections of coloured prints, usually accompanied by text, and where undertaken by an artist on a commercial basis for sale to the public.

The earliest of these was ***Norwich and the Broads*** published by Blackie and Son Limited in 1910 as part of their 'Beautiful England' series. This volume, as others in the series, consisted of twelve fine colour plates taken from watercolours painted by the artist Ernest Haslehust. There were also 56 pages of descriptive text, in this case written by Walter Jerrold. All the volumes in the series were bound in olive/buff card covers with the title etc in green and with a cut down illustration from one of the plates, within a green border, pasted onto the top board (in this case a view of Horning Ferry). The pages today are often subject to foxing and the spines prone to wear. The 'Beautiful England' series were sold in their thousands and the attractive 'period' Haslehust plates were frequently removed for framing, and also were copied by amateur artists. As well, there was a de luxe version issued bound in soft leather. Many titles in the series were republished after the second world war in a slighter binding with 'less sharp' colouring to the plates.

Perhaps as a result of the success that Blackie had with their 'Beautiful England' series, Jarrolds & Sons also entered this market and produced a series of books illustrated with colour plates from watercolours by (George) Parsons Norman. The text amounted to no more than about 30 to 40 pages and was unaccredited. The format and binding was almost identical to that used by Blackie down to using a similar coarse paper and a large dark type font. Jarrold's series included titles on Norwich and Poppyland as well as two separate volumes entitled ***Broadland*** which were published in 1912. Series I dealt with the northern rivers with the second series covering the southern ones including the section of the Broads situated in Suffolk. Jarrolds also published postcards from Parsons Norman's paintings and actually used these for the illustrations in the two broadland volumes. This form of illustration does tend to put strain on the spines of volumes so published, hence these are often found cracked or defective. The series was also published (in about equal numbers) in the traditional colour-plate form and these seem to have 'lasted' somewhat better. Jarrolds also projected volumes in this series on Aldeburgh and Caravanning, but I have found no evidence that they ever saw the light of day. In fact Parsons Norman had died, in his mid-seventies, at around the time of the outbreak of the first world war.

There were two other books, apparently privately published, from around this date. The first of these **Souvenir of The Broads** had no text and was in an oblong format with twelve postcard-sized colour plates, from original paintings by Warren Williams, tipped-in onto dark-grey thick paper. Printed beneath the plates were the locations which tend to be the popular visiting places, either from land or water. The brown thick paper covers had a view of Horning Ferry pasted onto the upper part with 'The Broads' impressed beneath. The book was bound with string ties. This publication, apparently for the tourist, probably did not sell in very large numbers and is seldom seen.

The other book, which came out probably a year or two before the first world war, was a far more impressive work. This was entitled **Pen and Pencil Sketches in Norfolk and Suffolk** by W Ayrton who was an artist and seemingly responsible for both the text and the colour plates, all of which were of broadland scenes. The oblong hardcovers, measuring 12" by 9½", opened to reveal a preface, list of the eight plates, and 13 pages of text by Ayrton extolling the natural delights of the Broads, all on fine paper with decorative borders. The views were: Barton Broad, Horning, Breydon Water, the Waveney, Rockland Broad and three of Hickling. These were to be found in a folder attached to the inside of the rear cover, each being tipped onto woven khaki card, and signed and dated between 1902 and 1911. The preface reads 'The coloured plates contained in the portfolio at the end have been specially reproduced from the original paintings of Mr W Ayrton, whose pictures of Broad and River Scenery are well known throughout the Eastern Counties'. The work was printed by William Clowes of London and Beccles but had no indication of a publisher and certainly would not have been cheap to produce. Copies are infrequently seen so it seems likely that this was a very expensive exercise by the artist!

Finally, though clearly privately produced, the work of Suffolk artist John Shewell Corder should perhaps also be included in this chapter. Corder was a contributor to Suffolk Archaeology and undertook works of architectural drawings in Ipswich and Bury St Edmunds. He was an accomplished artist and spent time sketching in broadland. He had a habit of reproducing his drawings lithographically onto thin card and forming small portfolios for presentation to friends and family such as: **Greetings 1903 from John S Corder** *This Card's a Bridge by which I send Greetings sincere to every friend*. More usually these portfolios were seasonal: **A Christmas Greeting for** ..... I have examples from 1910, 1913, 1914 and 1917. Within the illustrated and titled covers would be a number of his illustrations on card, loosely inserted, and which were sometimes bound with silk ties. Corder sketched in many parts of the country so by no means all of his portfolios are representative of the Broads. His **A Christmas Greeting for 1910** was subtitled **Hickling Sketches** and contained four illustrations of the area.

Potter Heigham bridge by John S Corder.

I have two copies of this title, one is dedicated to Harry Corder, the other to Norton Burroughes Garrard. ***Greetings 1903*** contained six illustrations namely: Horning Ferry, Waveney at Beccles, Haddiscoe, Potter Heigham, Ludham and Wroxham Bridge. There are probably other titles and dates still to be identified, particularly as I have noted several other single broadland views by Corder which may have been separated from such small portfolios.

FISHING ON THE RIVERS AND BROADS

The majority of general volumes in the 'coarse fishing on inland waters' ilk have a chapter, or at least a paragraph or two, about fishing in Norfolk and, in particular, the Broads. I do not feel that this book can do justice to a bibliography of volumes about fishing in English waters, so I have limited the content of this chapter to just a few specific titles.

As will be seen in a later chapter, with a view to selling tickets, railway companies were a great champion for promoting the Norfolk and Suffolk Broads. Publications extolling the attractions of the region came within the companies remit, and of course fishing was one of those attractions.

The early 1870s saw the co-operation of the publisher Horace Cox with Greville Barnes, the piscatorial correspondent to *The Field*, with the latter penning ***The Rail and The Rod or Tourist-Angler's Guide to many of the Waters and Quarters on the Great Eastern, Midland, London and North-Western, and Great Northern Railways***. This was published in six parts, No. VI (dated 1871) of which covered the waters in Norfolk including, among others, the Waveney, Bure, Yare and the Broads. The slim 84 page

GNR – Guide to Angling Resorts.

part volume was bound in plain green boards with a white label, on which was the title printed in black and pasted to the front cover. Individual parts could be purchased separately or all six bound as one volume.

The Great Northern Railway was also concerned with publishing tourist guides on this subject. Under their auspices, J H R Bazley in 1909 wrote **Guide to Angling Resorts** a 139 page angling guidebook divided into three headings: *The Rivers and Broads of Norfolk and Suffolk*, *The Waters of Lincolnshire Fens*, and *The Great Ouse*. To the rear of the volume were 30 pages of adverts, the majority relating to Norwich and Broadland. The GNR, like the GER, actively published numerous booklets extolling sport and recreation within the area in which their trains ran.

By far the most popular volume on this subject not unnaturally was published by Jarrold and Sons, and in various forms continued in print until the second world war. This was **The Illustrated Guide to Fishing in Norfolk Waters** *With full information as to Fishing Stations, Bait, River Distances, &c., &c.* Some issues had the prefix **Jarrolds'** but were otherwise largely identical in text and form. The first edition of this slim 112 page paper-covered guide was issued in 1889 under the authorship of Robert Moll. Clearly successful, several editions quickly followed with the fourth edition being dated 1893. Two formats have been noted, only differing with the covers – one in buff paper covers with the title and an illustration of a fish in black; the other in Bettesworth illustrated chromolitho covers with an illustration of the Ferryboat Inn, Horning, to the front cover. Most editions do differ internally with respect to the adverts and also some are undated or dated only via the railway adverts.

By the mid-1890s this guide had been expanded to 156 pages and described as a 'Revised Edition' (undated). Another edition, dated 1896, amounted to 158 pages with my copy containing a railway advert for 1900. Both editions were now under the authorship of A J Rudd, whose name was added in place of a crossed out Robert Moll, and published in Bettesworth covers. Cloth-covered editions with rounded corners, were also published at this time and were probably printed at the time that Rudd took over the authorship, rather than being a case of 'using up old stock' as with the paper-covered editions. By 1912 a rather more substantial 'Revised Edition' in thick illustrated printed boards was published, though with an identical number of pages. All the Jarrold's editions were rather ephemeral and are rarely seen today in anything other than in a somewhat defective state. As with many of Jarrold's publications, the publishing details were very confusing!

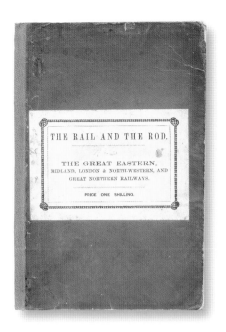

The Rail and the Rod.

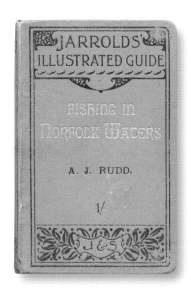

Fishing in Norfolk Waters.
1896.

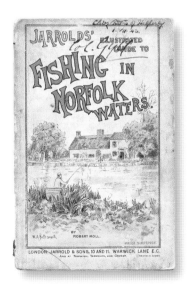

Jarrolds' Fishing in Norfolk
Waters. 1893. 4th edition.

Jarrolds' Fishing in Norfolk
Waters. 1912. Revised edition.

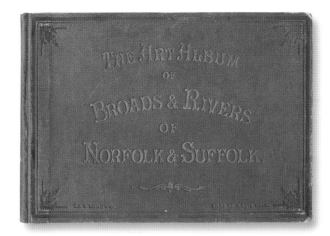

The Art Album of the Broads and Rivers of Norfolk & Suffolk.

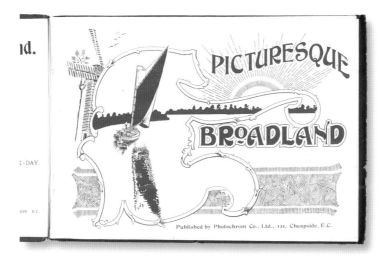

Picturesque Broadland.

Souvenir of the Broads by W Williams.

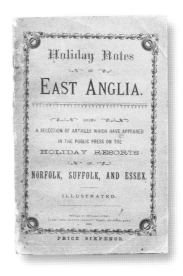

Great Northern Railway:
Sunny Norfolk

Holiday Notes in East Anglia
published by the Great
Eastern Railway.

An Ideal Holiday, the District of the Broads by Percy Lindley.

*M&GN Combined Tours of the
Norfolk Broads, 1910.*

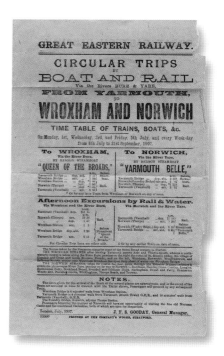

*Great Eastern Railway Circular
Trips by Boat and Rail, 1907.*

Folding GER Flyer, 1899.

SOUVENIRS
OF THE BROADS

In many respects the following books could have been placed with those described in the Painted Scene, other than that the illustrations tended to be derived from photographs taken of broadland scenes and then reproduced, rather than of works by named artists.

This category includes one of the Broads' most sought after books namely *'Norfolk Broads' Illustrated* by Colin Lunn. Priced at three shillings and sixpence and published in 1891, this oblong book had 13 pages of text which related to and described the twelve sepia real photographs, mounted on card, which comprised this volume, and which makes the book so desirable. The photographs were taken of Wroxham Bridge, Horning Ferry, Gorleston Harbour (two views), Acle Regatta (also repeated on the front cover), Lowestoft Harbour (two views), Hickling Broad, Gorleston Quay, St Benet's Abbey, Salhouse Broad and Heigham Sounds. In italics to the base of page 13, the author states *"Intending visitors to the Broads cannot do better than apply to Mr John Allen, of Coltishall, whose fleet, as the writer can vouch from his own personal experience, is both numerous and well found."*

'Norfolk Broads' was published by Simpkin, Marshall and Co and also by Jarrold and Sons.

Jarrolds also published in 1905 *Pictures in Colour of the Norfolk Broads with descriptive notes. Containing Fifty Beautifully Coloured Pictures.* Priced at 2s 6d with optional postage at 4d, this volume was the first of a series to be brought out by them illustrating and describing popular tourist districts, and aimed for purchase by the visitor. Other volumes in the series soon followed and included: Warwickshire and Shakespeare Country, Oxford University and also Cambridge University. One or two other areas were subsequently published in the same format and all are quite commonly seen. Tipped-in at the rear of the Broads' volume is a note stating that 'The Publishers of this Volume, Messrs Jarrold & Sons, Ltd., are prepared to undertake the printing

Flyer for 'Pictures in Colour of the Norfolk Broads'.

COLTISHALL LOCK.—Seven miles above Wroxham. The river Bure is worthy of all the praise which has been lavished upon it; at every bend of its course from Wroxham one is delighted with its freshness and distance from the turmoil of the outside world. The fishing is good here, and there are a number of Jack. In the spawning season the bream head up here in large numbers. The river is navigable for wherries and craft drawing little water for some eleven miles further up to Aylsham. Coltishall is accessible by rail also, being the next station to Wroxham.

NOTES . .   THE Rivers and Broads of Norfolk and Suffolk are particularly well situated for access from all parts of England. There are special Tourist and Yachting Tickets issued in connection with the G.E.R. and M. & G.N. Joint Railways from all ports of England all the year round. The Boating Station generally opens in the Easter of each year, and continues well on in October. As with all other holiday

Coltishall Lock from Jarrold's
Pictures of the Norfolk Broads.

of Coloured Books in this style for all parts of the world.' In their anonymous foreword, they state 'The reputation of the Broads of Norfolk is now far-famed, and as a holiday resort they are most deservedly popular. Herein we have endeavoured, with the aid of camera and skill of artist, to depict, in their natural colourings, a number of pictures of scenic beauty peculiar to this charming district; while the concise descriptive notes accompanying the views will, we hope, prove instructive and interesting to the visitor, without being tiresome'. This volume, as were others in the series, was attractively bound in two-tone cloth with a slim inset view, with the title of the book beneath, to one side of the front cover.

In about 1912 Jarrold & Sons undertook the publication of a similar quarto sized volume to that previously described, but now in sepia rather than colour, and with soft covers rather than hardback. Entitled ***Pictures of the Norfolk Broads*** *with Notes and Views of the Rivers Bure, Ant, Thurne, Yare, Waveney, &c.* this cheaper (1/-) volume was in a similar format and contained ninety-six rather grainy views from photographs, mostly of the Broads, together with descriptive text placed either above or below the view. There were also several pages of adverts including those for Jarrold's publications, boatyards, the GER and M&GNJR, as well as shops, hotels and boarding establishments. It is of interest that in a Publishers' Note it is stated that ' ....We therefore propose to issue a similar volume annually, and we shall therefore be *glad to receive* any suggestions or corrections to enable us to keep the volume up-to-date, also any photographs that may be sent us for publication in the forthcoming issue.' I am by no means certain that Jarrold's intention was adhered to, however, variants are noted. One such, undated and without advertising and with the same title, comprised only twelve of the views bound within printed card covers with a cloth spine. The publisher was stated as Jarrold & Sons Ltd, The Empire Press, Norwich, and the volume could well have been issued either just before or after the first world war.

In common with all districts that attracted the growing tourist trade, a number of souvenir books found their way onto stationers' bookshelves. They tended to be undated (to prolong shelve life) and oblong in style which best accommodated the 'landscape' photographic illustrations. The Broads were discovered too late for illustration in the 'Rock & Co' style steel-engraved view books of the 1860/70s (mostly these illustrated views were of the popular seaside resorts and historic cities) or in fact the glazed concertina-style souvenirs which followed a decade or so later. Around the turn of the century the popular style of souvenir tended to comprise a collection of photographic reproductions of the area, which in itself could be quite widespread and not always follow exactly that stated in the title, bound in usually red cloth or card bindings with no title page or other text, other than that stamped in gilt onto the top board. The sizes of the volumes could be anything from very small to quite large but approximately 9" x 6" perhaps being the most popular. ***The Art Album of Broads & Rivers of Norfolk & Suffolk*** was a typical example and comprised sixteen oblong photographic illustrations much in the Christoper Davies style. The publisher was E & S. from London who issued similar volumes for many other areas. Another publication, probably dating from the first decade of the twentieth century, was ***Picturesque Broadland*** which was produced by Photochrom Co Ltd, based in Cheapside, in East London. This was by far a more superior effort with fifteen photographic illustrations taken by the company itself, each with a few lines of description, two full page G E R advertisements and an artistic title page which was repeated in silver on the blue card covers.

   Souvenir of The Broads was yet another example of the genre. Undated (possibly published a few years before the first world war), without text other than a simple title in capitals to the brown paper covers, and with sixteen attractive tipped-in sepia views, this 10" x 8½" souvenir lacked any finesse whatsoever, nor any indication of a publisher or printer.

   Though I am sure that there are several other examples of view books yet to come to light, the final and most ephemeral example I will describe is ***Twenty Views of Norwich, Wroxham, and The Broads***. Geo Stephen, in his Broads' bibliography, dated this 7" x 4¾" slim booklet to 1914 though I am sure that it remained in print for many years after. It was published by the famous stationers W H Smith & Son of The Strand in London and sold for One Penny, probably in their own shops and on their bookstalls. The twenty black & white printed views, several of which are of scenes in Norwich, are contained within buff paper wraps overprinted in black with the title and price.

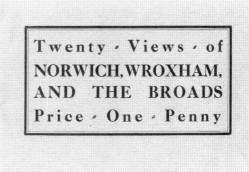

Twenty views of Norwich, Wroxham, and the Broads published by W H Smith & Son.

THE RAILWAYS

As discussed previously, the main nineteenth century railway companies were very effective in publicising the tourist aspects of their destinations. As far as Norfolk and Suffolk were concerned, it was in the promotion of the seaside resorts where the majority of the advertising budget was expended. The Broads, with its limited scope for mass leisure, tended to have only the odd chapter within publications which promoted the delights of visiting coastal East Anglia. Consequently, as with fishing, it is not possible to comprehensively describe the many volumes that promoted the area as a whole.

Mention has previously been made of John Payne Jennings' co-operation with the Great Eastern Railway. With its lines radiating eastwards from London, it was not unexpected that this sizeable and expansive company would dedicate a significant part of its advertising budget in the promotion of the attractions in East Anglia. Payne Jennings was a photographer and, as far as is known, did not write. Percy Lindley, however, was the reverse and edited many publications promoting the delights of this region, all of which emphasised the ease of travel by train, and the Great Eastern Railway in particular. Dating from the late 1880s right up until the GER was swallowed up by the LNER in 1923, Lindley published such titles as *Holidays in Eastern Counties*, *Summer Holidays*, *East Coast Pictures*, *On the East Coast*, *East Anglia Old and New* and so on. I have only one title, *Seaside and Countryside in East Anglia*, where it specifically stated that it was issued by the Great Eastern Railway (under the editorship of Percy Lindley). All these titles have the common thread of a description of the individual holiday resorts accompanied by absolutely superb period illustrations, mostly in colour, done by various artists of the time. It seems that nearly every year saw the publication of a different guide, and they

GNR – 'Twixt Thames and Tweed.

Published by the Great Northern Railway.

came out in all sorts of shapes, sizes and bindings. I have only seen one that is specific to the Broads, that being *An Ideal Holiday The District of the Broads*. This comprised 44 oblong pages within grey paper covers overprinted in white. The only advert is for H Blake & Co who advertise their hire boats for the 1915 season.

From at least 1886 until the early 1900s, the GER published, at their Stratford printing works, a series of booklets entitled *Holiday Notes in East Anglia*, and also *Holiday Haunts on the East Anglian Coast*, and these comprised series of articles that had previously appeared in periodicals such as the *Illustrated London News*, *The Pictorial World* as well as various local and national newspapers. The Broads was very well represented in these annuals, quite possibly because there were many articles to choose from with the district still being relatively newly discovered and extensively written about.

The Great Northern Railway also issued several booklets describing and advertising locations accessible from its core routes, as well as more general titles such as *'Twixt Thames & Tweed* which covered 'the East Coast Route' including the Broads. The Office of 'London of To-Day' published in 1898 a series of pamphlets called 'Holiday Leaflets Illustrated, Great Northern Series' of which No. 5 was entitled *Descriptive and Pictorial Account of Cromer, Sheringham, Mundesley, and The Broads* and edited by Charles Eyre Pascoe. About twenty years later, Great Northern Railway again turned their attentions to the area with a 16 page booklet called *Sunny Norfolk for Charming Holidays – Dickensland Poppyland Broadland*.

Bibliographies of books on the Broads mention other titles which I have not seen, including *Summer Holidays in the Land of the Broads* published by the Great Eastern Railway in 1893. In 1900 they also published *Waterways of Norfolk and Suffolk; with camp, yacht and canoe on the Norfolk Broads* by E Keble Chatterton which was illustrated with Payne Jennings' photographs. It is quite likely that there are several other ephemeral publications yet to be noted.

VERSE

Poetical anthologies have always been strong in the pastoral and poets, I am sure, have found little difficulty in being lyrically inspired by the Broads. Despite the title, ***Broadland and other Poems***, the contents of G F Bradby's slim 71 page 1904 published volume had only about one third of its contents based on this district. Godfrey Fox Bradby (1863–1947) was a poet with several published anthologies; he also wrote both fiction and non-fiction and his works included two novels based in broadland: ***Dick***, published in 1906, was an easy to read story about a schoolboy spending his summer holidays in a broadland cottage, with ***The Awakening of Bittlesham*** coming out the following year. Bradby clearly was a very popular author in those early decades of the twentieth century; ***Dick*** was reprinted three times before a cheaper edition surfaced in 1919. On the other hand, Hugh Money-Coutts in his ***The Broads 1919*** managed in verse to epitomise exactly what the Broads represented to so many visitors, or at least to those who survived the carnage of war that had taken place in the preceding years. This slim tall 27 page volume, bound in cloth-backed thick card boards and published the following year by The Bodley Head, has remained sought

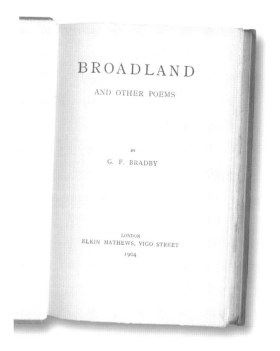

Title page from Broadland and Other Poems.

after not only by the collector of verse and volumes about broadland, but also to those who seek out works by the illustrator Donald Maxwell who provided the illustration for the coloured frontis.

> By Acle Bridge they slept; an aged dame,
>   Whose brains were nimble, though her legs were lame,
> Would sell them fowls, and cabbages. Next day
> They lowered the sail, the mast, and pushed their way
>   Shoulder to quant, with many a heave and groan,
>   Where sucked the tide beneath the well-worn stone,
> Then hoisted sail again; each quanting pole
> Long as the post which marks a Rugby goal,
>   Was laid in order by the fo'c'sle hatch
>   Starboard and port; ready for Dick to snatch
> (The wind being fowl) in toil to keep his weigh,
> So that Endeavour should her helm obey
>   When Ted, main-sheet in hand, hauled in the slack
>   Before he turned upon the starboard tack.
> For, sailing in a narrow water-way,
> When well to windward filch what ground you may;
>   And, if you are a Norfolk wherry-man,
>   Down the lee bank you steal what ground you can.

* The above verse appeared in Money-Coutts' The Broads 1919.

A FINAL VOLUME

World war naturally brought an end to the flood of books and guides, pamphlets and articles, catalogues and ephemera and so on, however, despite the conflict, surprisingly there was one final volume, published in 1915, and based on a holiday taken in that year on these waters. *A Holiday on the Broads or The Meanderings of 'The Moke'* was printed in Birmingham and edited by 'Flint', a member of the crew and who described himself as First Mate, Ship's Cook, Ship's Carpenter and Ship's Doctor, and who evidently had previously been more at home on the waters of the Avon. The other members of the crew were 'The Skipper' and 'The Ship's Boy', and the 'Moke' was their nickname for *The Reindeer* hired from Southgate's boatyard at Stalham and which had provided the accommodation for a holiday taken the previous year by The Skipper and Flint together with three other friends.

Their holiday commenced on Friday July 30th and, ending on August 14th, the book describes their day-to-day happenings and adventures, some of which was in accompaniment with the ladies on the *Wilhelmina*.

The 56 page unillustrated volume was attractively produced being bound in cloth-backed card boards with a simple cover in an art deco style. The book followed the pattern of previous 'our holiday on the Broads' works – factual but in a humorous style, nicknames for the hirers, many comments about the quirks of the locals and crew when hired, much description of eating and drinking and visits to farmhouses for milk and cheese, and finally the last day, return to the boatyard and journey home back to civilisation whence they came, usually by rail.

Considering that such books can be of very little interest to other than those who took part and their immediate family, it is not surprising that their circulation was so limited leading to their current rarity. However, they should not be decried; they tell us the type and social class that visited the district before the first world war, what they got up to, that they provided employment for the indigenous population, and very much how our district was seen through the eyes of others. Broadland literature would certainly be the poorer without them.

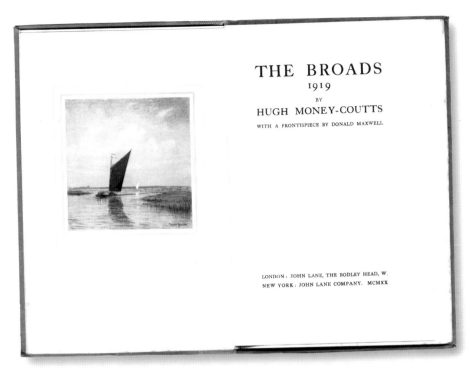

Frontispiece and title page of The Broads by Hugh Money-Coutts. 1919.

*Afloat on the Norfolk Broads
by Geo C Haite*

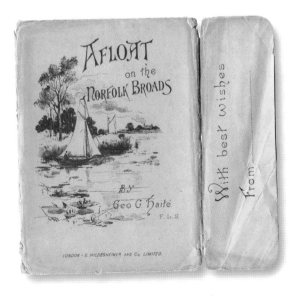

*Original paper envelope for
Afloat on the Norfolk Broads*

A FINAL VOLUME

A Holiday on the Broads, or the Meanderings of the 'Moke'.

WHAT ELSE IS THERE?

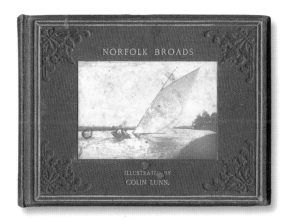

Norfolk Broads illustrated by Colin Lunn.

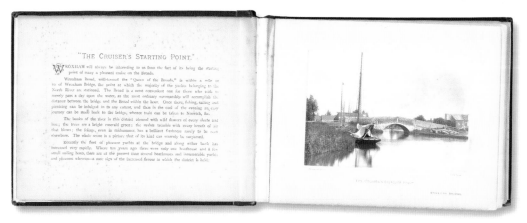

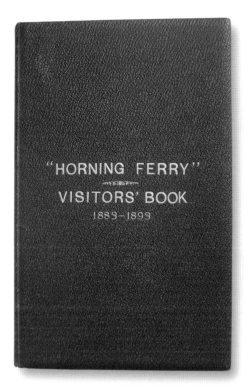

Horning Ferry Visitors' Book.

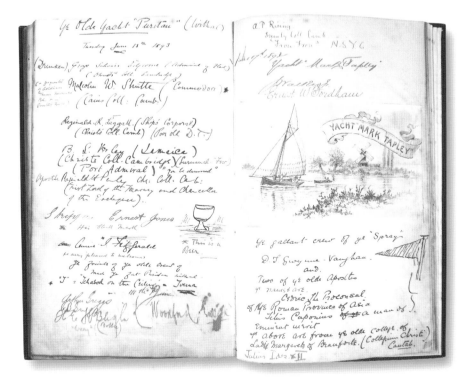

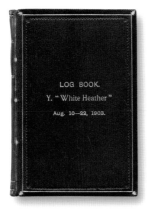

Log Book,
Y 'White Heather'
Aug 10–22, 1903.

1908 Blakes Yacht Hire catalogue (facsimile).

A J Caley & Son, Mineral Waters price list.

WHAT ELSE IS THERE?

As far as it has been possible, the preceding chapters comprehensively describe what may be termed as printed books with a substantial broadland content and that were written, or at least, published by the end of the first world war. What have I missed? In my twenty-five years of collecting 'Broads', I would like to say nothing, however, even the late David Ferrow ABA from Great Yarmouth, with about sixty-five years as a bookseller, from time to time came across volumes that he had previously never seen or, was in fact, even aware of. So to answer my own question, without any doubt unlisted books will surface infrequently, but it is a certainty that they will (as did the cheap edition of *On English Lagoons*). What would be their likely content – perhaps tales of early wherry or yachting holidays, Victorian or Edwardian novels, material published by or for the Great Eastern Railway and the Midland & Great Northern Joint Railway; as well there are sure to be souvenir or view books that I have yet to see. To prove my point, following an inspection of R C Fiske's collection at a very late stage in the writing of this bibliography, a finely printed slim octavo volume of only 25 pages came to my notice. Limited to fifty copies (this being number 13) and with a tipped in frontis plate of a yacht (presumably the *Blue Bird*), *The 'Blue Bird' among the Norfolk Reeds, with some reflections on the Water* was privately published in 1911 and written by Walter E Ledger. It goes without saying that this is extremely rare.

What have I excluded? My most obvious omission could be boat hire catalogues. This is a difficult category for any bibliography – most boatyards at some time or other issued their own catalogues before, or at the same time as, joining one of the hiring co-operatives. Most were thrown away and survivors are avidly collected. I have several dating from the 1930s, but before 1920 is another matter. Blakes commenced their operations in 1908 and the earliest I have

1896 cheap card bound edition of On English Lagoons.

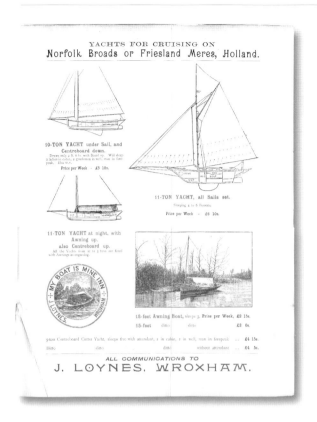

A page from John Loynes of Wroxham boat hire brochure.

dates from 1920 though earlier ones can be seen in facsimile. The Wroxham-based firm of George and English produced a 1914 season hire brochure which I have and I am sure that other yards also did including the pioneering John Loynes. I have an early undated fold-out brochure by him for hiring both on the Broads and the Friesland Meres, the latter being terminated by the onset of the Boer war. Hoseason, of course, did not commence operations until much later.

Manuscripts have not been included – they appear not infrequently – some written in exercise books, others elaborately produced accompanied by drawings and photographs and specially bound. By their very nature they are unique, but a few would have been used as a base for the privately printed 'our holiday on the Broads' books described in an earlier chapter. I mention three from my collection: ***Log Book. Y. 'White Heather' Aug. 10–22, 1903***, sumptuously bound in full blue calf with gilt tooling and lining with all page edges in gold. The 'skipper' was W H Elder, the 'Cook' L M Hobbs and 'Cabin Boy' G C Morgan, not forgetting Tenby the dog. The second, a more modest work but with several attractive sketches interspersing with the text – ***Cruiser Effendaitch, Log of the Watteau*** was commenced in 1908 and added to by several hands through the years until the last entry, dated Hickling 1914, subtitled *Three Weeks with the 'Watteau'*. What happened then-on; was it just the Great War that ended the years of leisure and pleasure, or did something far sadder take place in those fields of France and Flanders? The last, without title or names of the participants, was an oblong 'notebook' of 25 pages describing a holiday on the one and a half ton yacht the *Spree*. Written in narrative and very well illustrated with drawings of the yacht, their adventures and the places they visited, the sailing holiday started off on the 1st August 1895 from Brundall (following a short train journey from Norwich) and ended nine days later. Though in manuscript style, the text and drawings have been lithographically produced indicating that this is not the only copy:

St Benets is worth landing to look at and must have been a large Abbey in its day, as numerous cairns of old wall still testify. –
On the Monday morning the Commodore and Loafers having

(Above, and below) Two pages from a 1895 manuscript notebook relating to a holiday on the Broads.

"To those with whom I journeyed, I dedicate these serafs as a slight earnest of my thanks for the many kindnesses I received at their hands..." .... It seems probable that the writer's companions were each presented with a copy.

There is one person who specialised in producing mainly small, handwritten illustrated books about this area. That person, W H Cook, also produced manuscript newspapers for limited circulation, and his modest but attractive volumes often were

based on places such as Stalham and Eccles in East Norfolk as well as Ludham and St Benet's Abbey in broadland. For unique items, these are surprisingly frequently seen.

Like manuscripts, albums of photographs can also be considered as one offs. However, this is only part of the story as retailers such as Jarrold & Sons advertised the sale of series of photographs,

A massive album reputedly put together by Harry Brittain....

by such as Payne Jennings and Christopher Davies, in sets or for sale individually. Geo Stephen, the Norwich librarian, in his ***Books on the Broads a Chronological Bibliography***, which was published in 1921, also mentions a series of photographs by T Ayers mounted in an album, but perhaps this is also an one off. Publishers of photographs such as Frith and Valentine employed photographers who toured the more attractive parts of the land taking pictures from which many prints were taken and offered for sale. Albums, family or otherwise, would sometimes comprise some commercial photographs, such as these, interspersed with say holiday snaps. I have two massive albums, reputably put together by Harry Brittain, which charts the sailing of the wherry *Zoe* from Costessey and throughout the broadland river system. Of the hundreds of photographs in these albums, probably about half are from the lens of Christopher Davies, Payne Jennings and the London Stereoscopic and Photographic Company Limited, with the remainder privately taken.

Many guidebooks have a chapter or two describing the Broads; Stephen's bibliography mentions several including some primarily covering Yarmouth, Lowestoft and North Walsham. Apart from one or two that I have listed, the majority have been excluded on the grounds that they tend to add little that is new, are repetitive and that their reason d'etre is elsewhere. The same applies to some of the railway publications, many of which undertook the listing of holiday destinations and accommodation therein, so the inclusion of broadland would be almost certain in every edition.

Despite their often stunning piscatorial and aquatic artwork representative of the rivers and broads, I have not devoted a chapter to fishing menus. In 2008, Jamie

....charting the sailing of the wherry 'Zoe' on the broadland system.

Campbell undertook the publication of ***Norwich Angling Club Menus 1883–2008*** and this volume, still in print and obtainable from Jarrolds, reproduces and describes these in a far better manner than I am able. Whilst examples of these menus do turn up from time to time, the Norwich Angling Club was not the only fishing club to celebrate its dinners with such elaborate productions; others noted are from the St Andrews Angling Club and the Great Yarmouth Piscatorial Society. Sidney Howitt (1845–1915), an exhibitor with the Norwich Art Circle, was responsible for the artwork of many of the earlier menus, but illustrations from works by Frank Southgate and Arthur Patterson have also been noted.

Another manuscript source of broadland interest was the 'Visitors' book. These were sometimes seen at riverside hotels and inns, which attracted the tourist, yachtsman and traveller, and the paying guest was expected to pen a line or two of gratitude as to the accommodation provided or service given. These entries sometimes were expanded into verse or were accompanied by (not always) artistic sketches. ***The Horning Ferry Visitors' Book 1883–1893*** is packed with thousands of names with many familiar to the literature of broadland: early entries noted were by Harry Brittain on his yacht the *Buttercup* and Robert Moll (who described himself as correspondent to *The Fishing Gazette*) on the wherry *Hope*. Others included G Christopher Davies (sailing with the tenant farmer MP, Clare Sewell Read, in 1887 on the *Swan*), Jack Robinson, Ernest Tunbridge, Arthur Rackham and family, and so on. Rackham's entry included a caricature sketch, with signatures, of himself, his brother Harris and their friend William Ambrose together with their yacht *Young Rover*. Other well known names noted were Harry Blake, Loynes, Southgate, Rudd, Lunn and a Percival; as well there were several MPs, lords and ladies, Straceys, Gurneys, Birkbecks plus countless other names worthy of further research. Many entries included the name of the boat on which the visitor arrived and the *Buttercup* seemed to have been a very frequent visitor to the Ferry Inn. Wherries included the *Zoe, Maid of the Mist*, *Bertha*, *Diligent* and *Kate*.

Another visitors book, which dated from 1890 to 1910, was the ***Visitors Book, The Pleasure Boat Hickling***. This no less famous but less accessible inn also received thousands of visitors, however, with no recognisable names and many more yachts than wherries. Several entries praised George Beales, the landlord, and his wife and staff (particularly the 'fair Alice'). It is sad to recollect that as at 2009 both inns have spent periods tenantless and closed to the visitor.

Whilst booklets have found inclusion in the preceding chapters, magazine and newspaper articles have not. I think it near impossible to create a comprehensive list with Christopher Davies alone having penned seemingly hundreds. Some that appeared in such periodicals as ***the Graphic***, ***the Illustrated London News*** and ***the Illustrated Sporting and Dramatic News*** were often accompanied by fine wood engravings from sketches by such artists as Stanniland, and these have often been removed, hand-coloured and framed. Ephemeral railway timetables, printed by companies such as the Great Eastern Railway, were often produced for special holiday excursions to places such as Wroxham. Other ephemeral items included sale catalogues for farms, marshes and sometimes complete broads. A particularly fine example dating from July 1892 was for ***the Wroxham House Estate*** which advertised 123 building plots in the village itself. Its main interest as far as the Broads was concerned is that it contained three fine large lithographic views of the broad, the bridge and the river Bure as well as a large folding coloured plan showing the relationship of the estate with the river.

I will close this chapter by mentioning 'odd' volumes that were published perhaps primarily for the purpose of advertising. Page Brothers, the Norwich printing firm, brought out in 1895 a rather fine oblong book entitled ***East Anglian Health & Holiday Resorts, Illustrated. A Pictorial and Descriptive Guide for the Tourist or Visitor, the Student of Antiquity, and the Lover of the Picturesque***. Its 120 pages were packed with topographical interest, adverts and photographic reproductions. The Broads section, 14 pages long, detailed the district comprehensively as well as being illustrated with photos by Payne Jennings and others. It is very rarely seen so could not have been a commercial success. The Norwich food and drink company, A J Caley & Son, distributed a 12 page quarto sized ***Mineral Waters Price List*** which dated from around the turn of the century. This was beautifully illustrated with sepia coloured lithographic scenes from photographs taken by the Norwich photographer A E Coe of Broadland. Also the ladies and gentlemen's outfitters Mitchell and Hunter, based at Exchange Street in Norwich, produced around the turn of the century a thin 8 page advertising booklet of their wares, with for reasons not entirely clear five full-page wood engravings of scenes of the Broads. There are, I am certain, many other examples of advertising literature that have escaped my attention.

FURTHER READING

Geo Stephen's ***Books on the Broads a Chronological Bibliography*** is the only actual stand-alone bibliography ever published and which in any way provides a comprehensive listing of books written about the Broads. Published in 1921 as a 16 page booklet, its compilation was based on those volumes then contained within the City library and hence omits others that were not at hand therein. It was actually a reprint of the listing that had first appeared in a September 1921 edition of the *Norwich Mercury*. Stephen was for many years the head librarian for the corporation libraries with the main library, until its replacement in the 1960s, situated at Charing Cross. He published many such listings of books held by the city and also edited ***Readers' Guide, The Quarterly Magazine of the Norwich Public Libraries*** which was issued for many years. Volume VII, No. 3 in July 1918 included 'Arthur H Patterson: His Life and Writings, and a Bibliography,' and volume IX, No 14 in April 1929 had a fifteen page article 'Walter Rye, Benefactor to the Norwich Public Libraries' which included a comprehensive bibliography of books, pamphlets as well as articles written by him. This was also republished in the same year as a 32 page stand-alone booklet in commemoration of Rye, following his death. Walter Rye, of course, also published a bibliography of books on the broads in the appendix to his ***Songs, Stories and Sayings of Norfolk*** which was published by Agas H Goose in 1897.

The only comprehensive biography of books written by George Christopher Davies was published in 1999 by Jamie Campbell and the late Cliff Middleton. ***The Man who Found the Broads*** covered his life and writings as well as reproducing many photographs taken by him. Cliff Middleton also compiled ***The Broadland Photographers: The Photographs of J Payne Jennings, P H Emerson and George Christopher Davies***. This was published by Wensum Books in 1978 and is commonly found on the secondhand market. Following a 10 page introduction to the three photographers, the book continues with about eighty reproductions from their photographic works.

There are four books which describe Emerson's life and illustrate many of his photographs. The earliest (1974) was ***P H Emerson Photographer of Norfolk*** by Peter Turner and Richard Wood and which was published in the Gordon Fraser Photographic Monographs series. The following year saw the publication of ***P H Emerson, The Fight for Photography as a Fine Art*** by Nancy Newhall. This book was issued as volume 19 in the Aperture series and obtainable by subscription from New York. Like the following two volumes, it came out in an oblong format and comprised 266 pages of text and photographs. Up until very recently the most informative book, detailing

Emerson's work, and containing a bibliography, was the catalogue accompanying the 1986 Emerson exhibition – *Life and Landscape: P H Emerson Art & Photography in East Anglia 1885–1900* – which took place at the Sainsbury Centre at the University of East Anglia in Norwich. Chapters on various Emerson and Broadland subjects were contributed by such experts in the field* as Michael Brandon-Jones, David Cleveland, Cliff Middleton, Clive Wilkin-Jones and John Taylor. The last-named was also responsible for the most recent Emerson exhibition held in 2007 at the then named National Museum of Photography, Film and Television in Bradford. The accompanying hardback catalogue *The Old Order and The New P H Emerson and Photography 1885–1895* was also written by him and is the most academic of the four books that I have described. The exhibition was drawn from the collections both housed at the Museum and those of the Norfolk library collection held in the Forum, but also included items from the private libraries of John Benjafield, the Norfolk-based photographic researcher, and myself. From Bradford the exhibition travelled to the Getty and the Chrysler Museums in the United States. Regretably the Norfolk Museums service did not take the opportunity to take part by providing a venue.

Apart from that compiled by Geo Stephens, described above, the life and works of Arthur H Patterson have been the subject of three books. Two were written by the late Beryl Tooley, who was Patterson's great-granddaughter, and both contain much biographical information as well as a bibliography of the books and articles penned by Patterson. *John Knowlittle, The Life of the Yarmouth Naturalist Arthur Henry Patterson, ALS* was published by Wilson-Poole in 1985, and *Scribblings of a Yarmouth Naturalist* privately published in 2004. The latter is described as 'An edited selection from the writings of Arthur Henry Patterson, ALS (John Knowlitle)'. The third book, again biographical and with a bibliography and several full-page Patterson sketches, was *Broadland Naturalist, The Life of Arthur H Patterson, ALS ('John Knowlittle')* by Stanley A Manning and published by the Soman-Wherry Press Ltd in 1948.

The work of John Payne Jennings for the Great Eastern Railway with respect to railway carriage pictures is touched upon in the standard work on this subject *Landscapes under the Luggage Rack*, written by Greg Norden (1997 and subsequent editions). Jarrold & Sons have utilised reproductions from Payne Jenning's photographs in several of their travel books with some also including line drawings commissioned from the illustrator Arthur Rackham, who later became very famous for his fantasy colour book plates. Alison Barnes tells the story of Rackham's early work undertaken for Jarrolds in her book *Arthur Rackham in East Anglia* (2005). The majority of these commissions were for scenes of the East Anglian coast, but some were of the Broads, with three volumes being so illustrated: *Sunrise – Land* by Annie Berlyn (1894), being almost exclusively Rackham, *East Coast Scenery* by William Tate (1899) and *Pictures of East Coast Health Resorts* edited by Arthur Peaton (undated). The last two contain work by both Rackham and Payne Jennings.

E A (Ted) Ellis, the much missed and loved naturalist, penned *The Broads* in the 'New Naturalist' series published by Collins (1965 – No. 46). To the rear of this book he included a bibliography of books and articles written about the Broads, but very much related to Geology, Zoology and Botany. Its value lays in that listed were many early articles from scientific and specialist journals, in addition to the more commonly seen books.

This catalogue also includes bibliographies of books and articles written about the Broads up to the date of 1900.

A CHRONOLOGICAL LISTING

1826

J W ROBBERDS JUNIOR *Geological and Historical Observations of the Eastern Vallies of Norfolk.*

1830

FRANCIS STONE *Picturesque Views of all the Bridges belonging to the County of Norfolk*, in a series of 84 Prints in Lithography.

1834

J W ROBBERDS/JAMES STARK *Scenery of the Rivers of Norfolk comprising the Yare, the Waveney, and the Bure.*

1843

VARIOUS CONTRIBUTORS *The Zoologist: A Popular Miscellany of Natural History.* (Issued from 1843 until 1915).

1845

REV RICHARD LUBBOCK *Observations on the Fauna of Norfolk and more particularly on the District of the Broads.* (2nd Edition 1848, New Edition with notes by Thomas Southwell 1879).

1865

WALTER WHITE *Eastern England from the Thames to the Humber.* 2 Volumes.

1866

HENRY STEVENSON *The Birds of Norfolk.* (Volume 2, 1870; Volume 3, 1890 by Thomas Southwell).
WILKIE COLLINS *Armadale.* 2 Volumes.

1869

VARIOUS CONTRIBUTORS Transactions of the Norfolk and Norwich Naturalists' Society. (Published annually to date).

1870

JOHN MURRAY (published by) *Handbook for Essex, Suffolk, Norfolk and Cambridgeshire*. (Subsequent editions 1875 & 1892).

1871

C A CAMPLING *The Log of the Stranger, a Cruise on the Broads of Norfolk*.
GREVILLE BARNES *The Rail and the Rod*.

1872

C A CAMPLING *The Log of a Trip Taken in 1867 on the Rivers and Broads of Norfolk*.

1873

G C DAVIES *Mountain Meadow and Mere*.

1875

F BUCKLAND *Report on the Fisheries of Norfolk*.

1876

G C DAVIES *The Swan and her Crew*.

1882

G C DAVIES *The Handbook to the Rivers and Broads of Norfolk and Suffolk*.
W F *The Broads and Rivers of Norfolk*.

1883

G C DAVIES *Norfolk Broads and Rivers or the Waterways, Lagoons, and Decoys of East Anglia*. (New Edition 1884).
G C DAVIES *The Scenery of the Broads and Rivers of Norfolk and Suffolk*. (Part 1 and Part 2, each containing 24 loose photogravures).
R M N *A Week on the Broads*.
C S WARD *The Eastern Counties with a Practical Section on the Rivers and Broads*. (Through Guide series published by Thomas Nelson and Sons. Several Editions).

1884

H BRITTAIN *The Cruise of the Buttercup* (Published in the Holiday Annual).

1885

E R SUFFLING *The Land of the Broads*. (1st Illustrated Edition, published 1887).
H BRITTAIN *A Peep at the Broads, or a Corinthian Trip on the Bure and Thurn*. (Published in the Holiday Annual).
G C DAVIES *Norfolk Broad and River Fishing*. (In Volume 2, Fishing – Pike and other Coarse Fish, Badminton Library).

H BRITTAIN *14 Days Afloat*.

1886

GREAT EASTERN RAILWAY *Holiday Notes in East Anglia*. (Published in several
    forms over about twenty years).
E M HARVEY *The Cruise of the Kate*.

1887

H BRITTAIN *Notes on the Broads and Rivers of Norfolk and Suffolk*.
W RYE *A Month on the Norfolk Broads on board the Wherry Zoe and its Tender, the
    tub Lotus*.
P.H. EMERSON Life and Landscape on the Norfolk Broads. (Dated 1886).
P H EMERSON *Idyls of the Norfolk Broads*.
J F MOSTYN CLARKE *Three Weeks in Norfolk being a portion of the Rover Log*.
G C HAITE *Afloat on the Norfolk Broads*.

1889

R MOLL *The Illustrated Guide to Fishing in Norfolk Waters*.
P H EMERSON *English Idyls*. (Re-issued in 1924).
H M DOUGHTY *Summer in Broadland*.
G C DAVIES *The Scenery of the Rivers and Broads of Norfolk and Suffolk*. (The 48
    photogravures bound in one volume each with a page of brief description).
C E BRENNAN *Journal of a short Cruise on the Rivers and Broads of Norfolk and
    Suffolk*.
W SENIOR *The Rivers of East Anglia*. (In Rivers of the East Coast, volume 2).
F A KNIGHT *By Quiet Waters*. (In By Leafy Ways – Brief Studies from the Book of
    Nature).

1890

H BRITTAIN *Rambles in East Anglia*.
BLUE PETER *A Week in a Wherry on the Norfolk Broads*.
H M L *Rough Notes on Natural History in Norfolk and the Eastern Counties*.
DARLEY DALE *Noah's Ark*.

1891

E R SUFFLING *The History and Legends of the Broad District*.
E R SUFFLING *How to Organise a Cruise on the Broads*.
T W ELLIS *The Merry Mariner*.
C LUNN *Norfolk Broads*.
P H EMERSON *East Coast Yarns*.
J PAYNE JENNINGS *Sun Pictures of the Norfolk Broads*. (Published with text by
    E R Suffling in 1892, 3rd edition 1897).
E TUNBRIDGE *High Jinks, a Yarn of the Norfolk Broads*.

Rev M C H BIRD *Bird-Life of the Norfolk Broads*. (Published in The Field Club).
A GARDYNE *The Log of the Lalage*. (Previously published in Tinsley's magazine in 1889).

1892

W RYE *The Rights of Fishing, Shooting, and Sailing on the Norfolk Broads*.
COUNT D'EPREMESIUL *En Wherry*.
A H PATTERSON *Broadland Scribblings*.
P H EMERSON *Son of the Fens*.
W W SPELMAN (LUBERTA) *A Summer Sojourn on the East Coast*.

1893

W RYE *The Hickling Broad Case: Micklethwaite v. Vincent*.
GREAT EASTERN RAILWAY *Summer Holidays in the Land of the Broads*.
P H EMERSON *On English Lagoons*.

1894

H H WARNER *Holiday Tramps through Picturesque England & Wales*. (*c*1894).
G C DAVIES *Yachting on the Norfolk Broads*. (In Volume 2 Yachting, Badminton Library).

1895

C COLEMAN LAING *A Week on the Bure, Ant & Thurne*.
J BICKERDYKE *The Best Cruise on the Broads*.
A H PATTERSON *Man and Nature on the Broads*.
P H EMERSON *Marsh Leaves*. (Cheap edition 1898).
P H EMERSON *Birds Beast and Fishes of the Norfolk Broadland*.

1896

A BOWMAN DODD *On the Broads*. (Previously published in the Century Magazine).
A J RUDD *(Jarrolds) Illustrated Guide to Fishing in Norfolk Waters*.
G STABLES *The Cruise of the Rover Caravan*.

1897

W RYE *Songs, Stories and Sayings of Norfolk*.

1898

P H EMERSON *The English Emersons*.
W A DUTT *By Sea Marge, Marsh and Mere*.
C E PASCOE *Descriptive and Pictorial Account of Cromer, Sheringham, Mundesley and the Broads*. (Published for the Great Northern Railway).

1899

W A DUTT *Highways, Byways and Waterways of East Anglia*.

1900

F ZORN *Bunce, the Bobby and the Broads*.

H R DE SALIS *Norfolk Waterways*.

E KEBLE CHATTERTON *Waterways of Norfolk and Suffolk with Camp, Yacht and Canoe on the Norfolk Broads*. (Published for the Great Eastern Railway).

R DARLINGTON *The Norfolk Broads*. (Many issues noted).

E & S *The Art Album of Broads and Rivers of Norfolk and Suffolk*. (*c*1900).

1901

Dr H S LUNN *Yachting on the Norfolk Broads*.

E R SUFFLING *The Innocents on the Broads*.

1902

N EVERITT *Broadland Sport*.

QUATUOR CORANATI LODGE *Summer Outing – Norwich 3rd to 6th July 1902*.

VARIOUS *The Harrison Exhibition*. (Exhibition catalogue).

Sir T BROWNE & T SOUTHWELL *Notes and Letters on the Natural History of Norfolk more especially on the Birds and Fishes*.

1903

W A DUTT *Norfolk Broads*. (Editions also published 1905, 1923 & 1930).

J BLYTH *Juicy Joe, a Romance of the Norfolk Marshlands*.

A H PATTERSON & A H SMITH *Charles H Harrison, Broadland Artist*.

1904

N EVERITT *Told by Twilight*.

G F BRADBY *Broadland and other Poems*.

1905

JARROLD & SONS *Pictures in Colour of the Norfolk Broads*.

1906

G F BRADBY *Dick*.

1907

G F BRADBY *The Awakening of Bittlesham*.

E L TURNER & P H BAHR *The Home-Life of some Marsh Birds*.

1909

J H R BAZLEY *Guide to Angling Resorts*.

WARD LOCK *The Broads and Rivers of Norfolk and Suffolk*. (Also appeared in other titles. Published until the 1970s).

1910

O G READY *Life and Sport on the Norfolk Broads in the Golden Days*.
H C SHELLEY *Untrodden English Ways*.
E W HASLEHUST & W JERROLD *Norwich and the Broads*.
PHOTOCHROM CO LTD *Picturesque Broadland* (*c*1910).
ANON *Souvenir of the Broads*. (*c*1910).

1911

S J HOUSLEY *Comfort in Small Craft*.
W E LEDGER *The Blue Bird among the Norfolk Reeds*.

1912

PARSONS NORMAN Broadland; Series 1 and 2.
W WILLIAMS *Souvenir of the Broads*.
W AYRTON *Pen and Pencil Sketches in Norfolk and Suffolk*.
JARROLD & SONS *Pictures of the Norfolk Broads*. (*c*1912).

1914

W H SMITH & SON *Twenty Views of Norwich, Wroxham and the Broads*.
P LINDLEY *An Ideal Holiday, the District of the Broads*.
GREAT NORTHERN RAILWAY *Norfolk for charming Holidays – Dickensland Poppyland Broadland*. (*c*1914).

1915

FLINT *A Holiday on the Broads or the Meanderings of 'The Moke'*.

1919

Lt-Col R F LUSH *The Norfolk Broads Handbook*.

1920

H MONEY COUTTS *The Broads 1919*. (Illustration by Donald Maxwell).

1923

W A DUTT *A Guide to the Norfolk Broads*.

OTHER TITLES
BY THE SAME AUTHOR

The Country Houses of Norfolk, Part One: The Major Houses.

Written by David Clarke, and published by Geo R Reeve Ltd, Wymondham.

104 pages, A5, with 80 monochrome photographs.

ISBN: 0 900616 76 8

Price: £8.95

The Country Houses of Norfolk, Part Two: The Lost Houses.

Written by David Clarke, and published by Geo R Reeve Ltd, Wymondham.

120 pages, A5, with 81 monochrome photographs.

ISBN:978 0 900616 82 2

Price: £9.75

Both books can be obtained from most bookshops or the author adding £1 p&p. A third title in the *Norfolk Country Houses* series is in preparation and will be published in autumn 2010.